GREAT AUSTRALIAN AVIATION STORIES

Jim Haynes Before becoming a professional entertainer, Jim Haynes taught writing, literature, history and drama in schools and universities in Australia and the UK. He has two masters' degrees in literature, appears regularly on television and radio, and is the author of ten bestselling compilations of Australian stories and verse. Jim lives on top of a high-rise building overlooking Botany Bay and Sydney Airport. This book is his first collaboration with his sister, Jillian Dellit.

Jillian Dellit lives in Adelaide and has been a teacher, lecturer in children's literature, school principal and educational administrator. Born in Sydney and educated at Sydney Girls' High School, Sydney University and the University of South Australia, Jillian is currently director of a ten-government initiative for technology related change in Australian and New Zealand schools. She has an MA in information studies and is a platinum status frequent flyer.

GREAT AUSTRALIAN AVIATION STORIES

*Characters, pioneers, triumphs,
tragedies and near misses*

JIM HAYNES &
JILLIAN DELLIT

ABC
Books

Imperial measurements and currency have been retained where appropriate.
1.6 km = 1 mile
$2 = £1

Published by ABC Books for the
AUSTRALIAN BROADCASTING CORPORATION
GPO Box 9994 Sydney NSW 2001

First published in July 2006
Reprinted October 2006

The National Library of Australia Cataloguing-in-Publication entry
Haynes, Jim.
Great Australian aviation stories.

Bibliography.
ISBN 978 0 7333 1707 1.

1. Aeronautics - Australia - Anecdotes. I. Dellit, Jillian.
II. Title.

629.130994

Cover and internal design by Luke Causby, Blue Cork Design
Typeset in 11 on 15pt Goudy by Agave Creative Group
Printed and bound in Australia by Griffin Press

Cover images: *Top left:* The 'Southern Cross' *Vic Hall Collection, Narromine Aviation
Museum, Top right:* Nancy Bird-Walton and her Gipsy Moth plane *National Library of
Australia (nla.pic-vn3302813) Bottom: (left to right)* Smithy, T H McWilliams,
Charles Ulm and local man Harry Thrall at Narromine in 1929. The three pilots were
returning to Sydney in the 'Southern Cross' from being lost near Wyndham in W.A.

5 4 3 2

This book is dedicated
to the memory of our mother,
Sylvia Joyce Haynes (née Ray)
1925–1993

Contents

Introduction

When our mother was five, our grandfather took her to see 'Smithy' land at Mascot aerodrome, not far from where they lived in Coward Street Mascot. The excitement, wonder and historic significance of that outing stayed with her all her life.

When we first heard the story, we were two kids growing up in Botany where the airport was as much part of our world as swimming in Botany Bay, taking the tram to Sunday school, or watching the smoke billowing eternally from Bunnerong Power Station.

We thought church services everywhere paused for the planes to pass overhead during the sermon, and the way the crockery rattled in our auntie's dresser when planes passed over was one of the attractions of visiting her home in Wentworth Avenue, Mascot.

As we approached our high school years, Mum looked for a job to help with the expenses of uniforms and books. She jumped at the chance to work at the airport when Qantas was recruiting for its staff canteen. The lunchtime hours suited her and, by the time we got home from school, she would have a cup of tea and biscuits ready and we became the audience for her accounts of what the pilots and 'hosties' were saying and doing and where they were going.

We soon knew all about the history of Qantas and Ansett, what buildings were being erected and demolished, which planes were being retired or commissioned and what the changes were on the overseas flight menus.

Without our realising it, aviation was altering the landscape of our childhood. Woolwashes, tanneries and market gardens gave way to freight depots, hotels, access roads, parking stations and the ever extending runways.

One Sunday in 1959 Mum took us to see over the new plane, the Boeing 707, set to revolutionise the long haul routes with its high capacity and cruising speed of 960 km/h. We walked down the aisle and were confronted by the future; row on row of smart seats, little windows and the smell of new upholstery.

There was a dark side to living next to the airport and the bay, too. In 1961 during a violent rainstorm, Jim heard the Vickers Viscount, Ansett-ANA Flight 325, going down into the bay that we considered to be a part of our backyard. All fifteen on board died.

This book tells some of the stories that shaped Australian aviation, and indirectly affected our lives. Our grandfather, the World War I veteran who took our mother to see Smithy land in Sydney, was part of the last generation to know what it was like to live in a world without planes, airports or an aviation industry.

Most of our grandparents' generation was born before 12 November 1894, when an Australian, Lawrence Hargrave, flew 5 m (16 feet) in a sling seat attached to four of the box kites he had invented, proving flight was possible and providing a cornerstone for other inventors and pioneers.

Many of the young men who enlisted in the army in World War I saw the chance to join the flying corps as a wonderful piece of luck. They would never have had the chance to learn to fly back home on the farm or in their city jobs.

The majority of them died – in training, in battle, or just in the normal course of flying. The few who survived had mostly joined

Photographer Unknown Southern Cross Trans Pacific Flight

'... to see Smithy land in Sydney.' Section of the crowd that welcomed the Southern Cross.

the flying corps towards the end of the war, and nearly all of them wanted the chance to keep flying as civilians.

This small group became the foundation of the emerging aviation industry. They begged and borrowed money to purchase or lease surplus army planes after the war. They badgered governments for sponsorship. They dreamed of flying home instead of a slow return by troopship. Kingsford Smith, Ulm, the Smith brothers and Hinkler all learned to fly during the war. Francis Briggs, the pilot in both the 'Flight to Alice' and 'Adelaide to Sydney' stories in this book, was also a World War I veteran. He was the pilot who flew Billy Hughes, the Australian prime minister, to the Paris peace talks at Versailles at the end of the war.

The Australian government had an inkling of the future possibilities when it offered a £10 000 reward for the fastest flight to Australia. The incentive worked. This was an opportunity for Australian servicemen still in Europe to keep flying and return home.

Mail routes, charter flights, flying schools, air shows, aerodromes and workshops all sprang up thanks to these returned servicemen–aviators. Few of them got rich, but mostly they earned enough to keep flying. Kingsford Smith spent much of his time chasing enough money to finance his next long distance flight.

Fortunately for us, writing accounts of their flights was one way they had of making a little money, so we have a legacy of first hand descriptions of their adventures.

Ross Smith's evocative account of the England to France leg of his historic flight captures the magic and wonder of flying above the clouds at a time when a mere handful of human beings had ever done it. Kingsford Smith's story of struggle and setback turning to achievement and euphoria is inspirational despite, or perhaps because of, its disarming matter-of-factness and modesty.

Between the wars civilians became excited by the idea of aviation, often through the enthusiasm and example of the veteran aviators. When, in 1925, the de Havilland company manufactured a simple, serviceable light plane, the Gipsy Moth, it opened up opportunities for solo flying. An enterprising doctor in Darwin bought one to reach his patients and, soon after, the Bush Church Aid Society in Ceduna, South Australia and the Australian Inland Mission in Cloncurry, Queensland, set up the services that grew into the Flying Doctor Service.

Pilots like Briggs established mail services, and the seeds of tourism were sown by journalists like Francis Birtles, who chartered planes to go to places such as Alice Springs so he could write about the experience for a newspaper.

Records were made and broken. Aviators arrived in Australia and made our country seem less isolated. Heroes like Smithy and Hinkler, and Amy Johnson, the 'lone girl flyer', gave inspiration, hope and a sense of wonder to a world in the Depression. And their stories sold newspapers.

Most of the pioneering aviators died young. There were none of the safety measures we take for granted. All our knowledge of aviation is based on the risks they took.

Some lucky ones, like Nancy Bird, lived to tell their stories and play a major part in the development of the aviation industry.

It took another war to give us a new generation of technology, engineers and planes that could reliably carry large numbers over great distances. After World War II aviation literally 'took off'.

Today we take a plane to go to work, or to go on a holiday, to attend a wedding, a funeral, a birthday dinner or a reunion. Our luggage is scanned, transported, loaded and unloaded. We are met by taxis or leave our car at the airport or take a train. We buy coffee and sandwiches – or franchised doughnuts – t-shirts for the kids and books to read on the flight if we don't want to watch the movie. If we are frail or our knees give out, we request a people mover to take us from the security gate to the plane, and most of our airports have air bridges to keep us off the tarmac.

We expect airlines to predict arrival times to the minute and planes to land on time. We travel to the USA without a stop and to Europe with only one stop.

In airports all around the country, men and women are employed in all types of work that enables them to give their children an education and opportunities, just as our mum did by working, first in the staff kitchens and later in the offices at Qantas, for nearly half her life.

Putting this book together has given us renewed respect for our mum's stories and rekindled a sense of awe and wonder at the achievements and heroism of Australia's aviation pioneers. What they did was remarkable and some of them were also remarkable storytellers.

These days most people have an aviation story to tell, because the vision, courage and daring of the people whose stories appear in this book gave us all the opportunity to fly.

Jillian Dellit & Jim Haynes
March 2006

GREAT AUSTRALIAN AVIATION STORIES

PART I

'INTO THE EMPTY SKIES' – OUTBACK AVIATION

Of all the continents, Australia is the most barren and hostile in terms of its terrain. Beyond the fertile coastal fringes, Australia has a sparse, well-scattered population. Aviation was always going to be a boon to the people of the outback; it was also always going to be fraught with the dangers and difficulties that isolation and a barren and inhospitable country presented.

The stories in this section demonstrate those special qualities we have come to expect from people who call the outback home, endurance and perseverance, mixed with a laconic acceptance of the way things are west of the Great Divide.

Here you will find the story of Nancy Bird's tenacity along with brief accounts of the achievements of people like John Flynn and Hudson Fysh who spent a large part of their lives helping to conquer the inhospitable and difficult landscape in order to bring aspects of civilization such as mail, medical aid and regular transport links to the remotest outposts of settlement.

The sense of wonder and novelty which is to be found in some of the journalistic accounts of early flights into the centre and intercity mail runs gives us a feel for the way flying was seen to be opening a whole new world of communication and contact between our widespread settled areas.

The wonderful old flying machines in these seventy-five-year-old stories take us all on a journey back in time and give the reader a taste of the mood of the time. In these stories we get a sense of the optimism and 'modernity' which permeated the early years of commercial aviation in Australia.

First Flight to Alice, 1921

Francis Birtles

After many years of Australian overlanding I have discovered a new world – the loneliness of vast eternal spaces.

Although it is a lonely world, it is a roaring world, with never-ceasing, rushing gales, rolling masses of woolly clouds, and, down through deep aerial crevices, fleeting glimpses of white-specked cities, ribbons of tracks, and rivers weaving in and along dark blue masses of earth.

And there is a new tribe. They are youthful, capable men, strapped to and controlling a balanced roaring dragon of the air.

On earth these are men of quiet manner and volatile temperament. A strong distinguishing factor of this tribe is the smell of castor oil, with which they anoint themselves when in midair. Their eyeballs are slightly flattened out, owing to enormous wind pressure. Their nostrils are thin, owing to contraction keeping out the surplus supplies of air forced into their lungs. Their lips are tightset and their ears are not attuned to the slighter sounds on earth, as the drums have toughened owing to the everlasting thundering of engines and rushing of winds.

Lieutenant Briggs, the pilot, is a very young man, and anxious to avoid press publicity. George Bailey, the mechanic, is also a very young man. He is perfectly happy when he has a spanner in one pocket and an oil can in the other.

The mechanic is called in aviation circles the 'ground engineer', but should the engine 'cut out' when a mile or two above the earth he is sometimes called something else.

To begin the journey, we went roaring along on the aerial track from Melbourne to Adelaide.

In a mere half an hour a city glides past, and below is Ballarat. Banking steeply, the plane gives an airman's 'goodbye'. We are 3000 feet up, and travelling at 110 miles an hour against a headwind.

Down below, the country is thickly pockmarked. There are thousands of circular, dark holes, with a fringe of light earth around, a reminder of early day goldseekers' efforts. There are also green carpets, with fancy stripes; chocolate carpets, square and oblong, spotted with green; red tiled floors with zig zaggy streaks; and all kinds of queer geometrical patterns, unwittingly made by farmers in their cultivation paddocks.

For scores of miles we race along over these settled areas.

Down below, the rolling hills, like petrified waves, are creating air pockets and air disturbances. A few yards overhead dark gloomy clouds streak by. Rolling over and over between the breaks is a tumbling mass of silvery woolly clouds. A big rainbow hangs dimly over all.

Suddenly the aeroplane ducks and dives. A big eagle has swooped down. Pilot Briggs has sighted him coming. With the feathers on his throat standing stiffly out, and his neck waggling indignantly, the bird zooms upward into a misty cloud. Gaining height, he charges down again, and misses by half a mile astern. After us he comes, but he seems to be flying backwards. Over 100 miles an hour is too fast for him.

There are more air bumps; more eagles trailing hopelessly behind us for a moment, before they are gone into the swirling mists.

Soon we are crossing the tail end of the Grampians and away in the far blue distance a white spot gleams. It is the Nhill silo, 100 miles away, between stern granite clad passages, up which we fly.

There are more bumps and wisps of white clouds scurrying by, going like scalded cats. Then a wonderful panorama of tree clad hills, little paddocks, miniature farmhouses, and streaks of water drift by.

Soon we are heaving and swinging along over the Ninety Mile Desert, following a lone white thread below, with a little black grub crawling along on it. It is an express train on the Adelaide railway line.

We cross above rolling sand waves stilled by unseen powers, desert sand hills, then more fancywork carpeted paddocks and the golden gleam of the waters of the Cooyong, seemingly suspended in midair.

Then comes a canal with scattered habitations clinging to its banks. It is the Murray River, and in flood, too. White, frightened pelicans huddle closely together on outlying pools; wild ducks upend hastily and dive below muddy waters.

Our aerial dragon now mounts higher and higher. There are glorious sunset cloud effects. Then come the dark masses of the Mount Lofty Ranges. An extra high spur glides by rapidly a few hundred feet below. Then another, and another.

Little dolls' houses are now dotted about, perched on the edges of gloomy verdure clad slopes. On a long glide we nose down the slopes, then, banking steeply, we gaze down into and between the spires and buildings of Adelaide.

On leaving Adelaide after rest and refuelling, we ran into rain squalls and storms. The tremendous backdraught from the propellers blew the rain away from the sheltering cowls, behind which we crouched, and hailstones, like thousands of little dervishes, danced about on the taut green wing planes.

The aeroplane tore through the black cloud and broke out into brilliant sunshine. At Carrieton we landed and lunched at a shearer's hut – with all the population of the countryside gathered there to see us.

As we cut across country to Hawker, a world of everchanging blue lay below us.

Passing over a wave shaped spur of the magnificent Flinders Ranges, we bumped into a swirling air pocket. The plane made a half-spin and dropped sharply, our luggage nearly going overboard. Mile upon mile of mountain country lay east and west, and suddenly the engine cut out. A swift nosedive and three thousand feet below was the earth!

The earth rushed up to meet us straight over a tree-lined watercourse, with the tops of trees close by underneath.

Ahead was a little table top plateau. A quick side swing of the plane and whoosh, swish, bumps and jumps! Bushes and small stones scattered in all directions and a startled rabbit accelerated rapidly from a saltbush.

We were down. On a dry stage, and no water in sight.

As the engine and exhaust pipes cooled off, we sat underneath the shade of the wings. Then the engine was inspected and Bailey went to work.

One of the carburettors had been flooding badly but it was not a serious problem and in the afternoon we got away again. By evening we had landed on a stony plain at Maree and we camped there at the local hotel.

Out on the plains stood our frail looking chariot – a graceful light thing of wood and linen, pegged down and riding out a gale of dust and wind.

Around it several donkeys and one inquisitive camel stood in respectful admiration. A billy goat, more practical, licked the castor oil from the greasy fuselage. Underneath the wingtips stood his wife, eating a fluttering newspaper – a literary goat 'devouring the news of the day'.

During the evening we read the weekly papers and discussed the agricultural, stock and beekeeping columns, and then to bunk. Dreamily we talked of snakes and other luxuries.

From the next room came sniffling cries, which soon increased to prolonged howls, from a two-year-old. Then came a woman's lullaby song, and curses from a sleepy father.

Soon after there came snores from Briggs and Bailey.

Clatter, bang, rattle! Bailey had fallen out of bed! His foot had come in contact with some cold toilet articles which Briggs and I had thoughtfully hidden between his sheets. The talk of snakes had done the rest.

Next day we flew across the end of the South Lake Eyre, but no water was in sight. There was a vast, gleaming expanse of white salt, fading away into blue distance.

We were three solitary voyagers, in the lonely air spaces above Central Australia, roaring along over the scenes of the hardships and tragedies of early day desert explorers.

Down below the effect was like that of an old, grey-red carpet splashed with green and yellow. Little blue pinpoints here and there denoted small waterholes. The early morning was calm, and through the glassy atmosphere, so still and so crisp, our powerful plane bore along steadily.

A few minutes before reaching Oodnadatta, we gathered about us an escort of all the hawks and crows in the district, and they followed us right over the town, which provided a most unique and amusing spectacle for the residents below, who had assembled to see us land.

The DH4, was the first aeroplane to land at the railhead, and the first to penetrate so far north towards the centre of Australia. Our flying time from Maree was two hours twenty minutes.

We spent a day at Oodnadatta.

Like Maree, the country surrounding the town is bare of much vegetation and covered with small smooth stones from the size of a marble to a cricket ball. When we landed and took off again these stones shot out from beneath the tyres like shrapnel, and with considerable force.

We left on the morning of 4 October for Charlotte Waters, NT. Again the whole township turned out to see us off, despite the early hour of six am.

I could not help thinking and hoping that the present interest evinced would some day be nullified by the departure of airliners as frequently as ocean liners from our ports today. Air transport must and will grow to become the national asset that the merchant service already is.

To Charlotte Waters, 120 miles away, my only guide was the camel pad, the telegraph line, and a knowledge that the place was about due north. For the first twenty miles the telegraph line and camel pad ran together. My original intention was to follow the telegraph line as it was most direct, but when it left the pad I could not see it sufficiently well to follow, so I felt my way back to the pad and followed that.

The pad went nearly north and crossed the river Alberga at the junction of that stream and the river Stevenson (or Ooljeraginia). Just after the junction, we passed over Macumba Homestead. The pad then follows up the right bank of the Stevenson for some fifty miles, passing through Willow Well, from where another track branches away to the right to run out to Dalhousie Homestead, then back to join the pad I was following. At Blood Creek, on the Oolarbarrinna Waterhole and Hamilton Creek Bore, the Hamilton flows (when it does flow) into the Stevenson.

At the junction I could see a lone homestead. The river and camel pad gradually work round to the north-west until they meet the telegraph line which runs more or less parallel to the river, and a few miles to the west.

The line and pad then continue north, and the Stevenson turns away west to its source. A short run brought us over Blood's Creek Homestead, with Charlotte Waters Telegraph Station sighted in the distance.

A few minutes flying brought us over our destination to a safe landing. We were welcomed by the only white men there, two gentlemen of the telegraph station staff, who at once made us at home.

The other residents of the place also gathered to see us land, but some of the wilder and more timid ones went bush and hid when they first heard and saw us. Later they recovered sufficient courage to approach the 'big eagle-hawk' as they termed the machine.

Our flying time from Oodnadatta was one hour fifteen minutes. The rivers I mentioned were merely sandy beds with occasional waterholes.

The country till now had a very bare appearance, but at Charlotte Waters the country suddenly changes to thick scrub. The change is so abrupt and definite that it looks as though a line has been drawn to define where one should finish and the other start.

I noticed a similar definite change of country when I flew to Perth. The Nullarbor Plain starts and finishes from scrub country in the same way.

We were in the air much too early in the morning to catch any camel trains or transport on the pad, but I observed a few camps stirring beside the way, mostly near waterholes.

We left Charlotte Waters on 5 October at 6.45 am, on the last stage to Alice Springs.

Pilot Briggs, seated in the cockpit, was soon waggling the joystick, signalling to us. Ahead, below, through the taut rigging, and between the ever outstretched wings, was a glorious panorama. Thousands of square miles of scrub dotted plains melted into deep blue mysteries of unexplored lands. Vision by vision a winding S shaped series of white loops, varied by peculiar flat topped, curved, and cone foundations, was disclosed. These were the Finke River and the surrounding mountains, showing the effect of glacial erosion which had taken place ages ago.

On and on we went.

Snuggling at the foot of red and white hills in the bend of a river were the miniature houses and paddocks of the Horseshoe Bend Cattle Station.

Here microscopic human beings stood stockstill, and antlike horses scampered into mobs. Banking over and over, with its wingtips pointing straight to earth, the aeroplane gave its greetings to those below. From over the fuselage a letter dropped, the attached 50 foot red, white and blue streamer waving gracefully as it unrolled on its downward flight.

The sun blazed out redly through dark clouds and we bumped, we swung, we heaved, we swirled, we dived, and we rose. We were passing over a ruddy-yellow series of spinifex-clad undulations – the notorious Depot Sandhills – every one of which was giving out its own particular variety of air current. With my right shoulder jammed under a bracing wire, I was engaged in photographing and making rough pencil charts.

Another wriggle of the plane, and we saw a long string of camels plodding along. They were some six weeks out from the place we had left that very morning.

As we watched them we plunged into a vicious air pocket, and a vile smelling, swirling spray of burnt castor oil came from the engine exhausts. Sniffing it out hastily, I breathed in short respirations and then sat tight. The plains below us were now blackened from grassfires.

Delicate traceries of white denoted where trees had been burnt to ashes, trunk, branches, and limbs being clearly outlined in white, while the skeleton tracery of a burnt camel could be clearly seen.

Signal smoke fires on a burnt patch of ground denoted our chosen landing place at Alice Springs, and little white specks of human beings on a rocky ridge moved about.

On a long glide the machine descended with its engine throttled back, then gave out a roar of power as we swept along over the fleeting treetops. With us rested the satisfaction of pioneering an air route to the very heart of Australia.

The countryside whizzed by us as we descended; then, with a gentle bump and raising a swirling cloud of dust, we landed.

EDITORS' NOTE: On 21 September 1921 Francis Birtles, the famous overlander, commissioned the pioneer aviator Francis Briggs to fly him from Melbourne to Alice Springs via Adelaide. It was the first flight ever to Alice Springs. Birtles served in the Boer War and had been a mounted police officer in the Transvaal. He cycled around Australia twice and crossed Australia seven times before 1912. In 1912 he was the first person to cross from Fremantle to Sydney by car. He competed in seventy transcontinental car races, many of which he wrote about and filmed.

The Little Town that Took Off

Jim Haynes

Being on a direct line of flight from Darwin to Sydney was a happy geographic coincidence that was to help the little town of Narromine, in western New South Wales, play a big role in Australian aviation history. But it was the enthusiasm and hospitality of its people that gave this little town a special place in the hearts of aviators and aviation enthusiasts worldwide.

Once powered flight became a reality, people who lived in isolation were quick to seize on the idea of flying as a means of transport. The fascination with flying had spread quickly through the rural areas of Australia within a few short years of the Wright brothers' pioneering flights of 1903 to 1905.

Out near the small town of Narromine, around World War I, a young farmer named Jim Hayden decided to experiment. He eventually built a Bleriot-type monoplane at his property, 'Acton', the first aircraft to be seen in the Narromine district. Apparently,

Narromine Aviation Museum

'… *the first aircraft to be seen in the Narromine district.' Jim Hayden's
Bleriot-type monoplane.*

it was nose heavy and probably never flew, although it was
displayed at the Narromine show.

Jim's son Keith (an airframe fitter at Narromine during World
War II) still remembers the plane, but, unfortunately, it didn't
survive the years.

What did survive the years, however, was the Hayden family's
fascination with building flying machines.

If we fast forward almost one hundred years from Jim Hayden's
plane building experiment, we find a Wright Model 'A' Flyer
replica being built at Narromine Aerodrome by the members of
the Hayden family and other local enthusiasts.

Hundreds of visitors to Hangar 10 at the aerodrome watched the
progress of this fascinating project for over a year and, in October
2005, thousands gathered at the Narromine Air Show to see the
replica fly. The guest of honour was Buzz Aldrin, the second man
to walk on the moon.

The Model 'A' was the Wrights' first practical aircraft, in the
sense that it could stay aloft as long as its fuel lasted and was fully
controllable. One Model 'A' even made a return trip across the

English Channel. The locally made, fully functional replica became one of a long list of famous aircraft to be associated with Narromine.

You see, the town of Narromine is now a famous centre for aviation heritage, with a very modern museum of aviation history and a long and distinguished history of achievements in aviation. Many families in the district have, like the Haydens, a proud tradition of three or more generations' involvement with aviation.

The very first entry in the logbook of Narromine Aerodrome records that an Australian Flying Corps BE2E landed on 20 November 1919.

Piloted by Captain Wrigley DFC with mechanic Lieutenant Murphy AFC DFC, the aircraft was on its way to Darwin to greet and escort Ross and Keith Smith and their crew, winners of the England to Australia air race.

The second entry, on 13 February 1920, is the Vickers Vimy G-EAOU. Piloted by Ross and Keith Smith, with sergeants Shiers and Bennett as crew. This was, of course, the famous 'God 'Elp All

Narromine Aviation Museum

'The second entry ... in the logbook of Narromine Aerodrome, on 13 February 1920, is the Vickers Vimy G-EAOU ... the first plane to fly from Britain to Australia.'

of Us', the first plane to fly from Britain to Australia and the winner of the great air race of 1919.

Nine years later, in September 1929, the Narromine Aero Club was formed at a public meeting. Possibly Australia's first regional aero club, its first president was Tom Perry, who had provided a paddock of his property, close to the town, to be developed as an aerodrome.

By October 1930, when the club held its first AGM, there was much to report. When the club had been formed one year previously, it had just twelve members; the club now had 200 members and what a year it had been!

In that first year of the aero club's existence, seventy aircraft had visited Narromine. Among them had been the *Southern Cross*, returning with Smithy and crew from being lost near Wyndham in Western Australia; the famous de Havilland DH61 *Canberra*, piloted by Les Holden, who had found the missing *Southern Cross*, Francis Chichester's famous Gipsy Moth on its record breaking solo flight from Britain; and the planes piloted by Bardsley, Wedgewood and Annabel on their round Australia flight.

All these pilots had been welcomed and given hospitality and help by the Narromine Aero Club. Many were also given civic receptions by the mayor and local council.

The most thrilling event of the first year had, however, been the staging of Narromine's first air pageant.

Some idea of the incredible interest in aviation at the time, and in the district, can be gained by looking at the figures recorded by the aero club for the air pageant held on that April weekend of 1930 at Narromine.

There were over a thousand cars at the airfield on the Sunday alone and over 5000 people paid 2s each, or 6d per child, to attend the show. There they witnessed the modern marvel of powered flight demonstrated in such entertaining events as formation flying, aerobatics and the amateur pilots' handicap.

To make sure the day contained enough entertainment for the general public, the aero club also included in the program

'All these pilots had been welcomed and given hospitality …' Southern Cross with townspeople and crew, 1932.

'Narromine's first Air Pageant' DH60 Moths and DH61 Giant Moth 'Canberra' at the 1930 Air Pageant.

demonstrations of such things as aerial combat, balloon strafing, crazy flying, bombing motorcars and a parachute drop!

Gate takings were a massive £420 and the Narromine Aero Club, which was just six months old at that point, had an enormously popular and successful event on its hands. Another pageant was planned for Easter 1931.

The following year the club was disappointed when several prominent aviators who had planned to attend the second pageant, among them Smithy and Major de Havilland, were unable to come. Both pilot numbers and attendances were down on the previous year, but the event still attracted over 3500 people in 500 cars, and the extra profits from a dance and joyrides took the takings to a similar figure to the previous year.

This was during the very depths of the Great Depression and what this little town was achieving in terms of event management, civic progress and promotion was truly remarkable.

Two further very successful air pageants were held at Narromine before the outbreak of World War II. At the 1935 pageant a young pilot named Nancy Bird won second prize in the main event. Later, Nancy often used the Narromine airfield during her pioneering work with the Far West Children's Health Scheme during the late 1930s, and it was a local grazier, philanthropist and aero club president, Tom Perry, who stepped in when Nancy needed help to obtain a more suitable plane for her work. Without his guarantee Nancy could not have secured the insurance she needed to get the loan for the aircraft.

Nancy Bird's connection with Narromine has continued to the present day and she was there in 2002, as an honoured guest, to officially open the Narromine Aviation Museum.

At the 1938 pageant, another female flyer was the winner of the newly instituted 'Arrival Race'. Entrants had to fly from their various home aero clubs and arrive as soon as possible after 11 am. Clare Thompson flew her Tiger Moth all the way from Melbourne and timed her arrival to cross the line at exactly one quarter of a minute after 11 am!

Other milestones through that period included a civic reception for famous New Zealand flyer Jean Batten, fresh from her record breaking flight from London to Darwin in May 1934, and the arrival of the first air mail, piloted by the great aviation pioneer Arthur Butler,* in December of the same year.

* EDITORS' NOTE: Cecil Arthur Butler (1902–80) was founder of Butler Air Transport (later Airlines of NSW). He designed, constructed and air tested the first all metal aircraft to be designed and flown in Australia in 1930 and broke the England–Australia flight record in 1931.

Narromine Aviation Museum

'... *famous New Zealand flyer, Jean Batten, fresh from her record breaking flight from London to Darwin in May of 1934.*'

The big aviation event of 1934, however, was the famous MacRobertson Centenary Air Race from London to Melbourne. Again, Narromine was right in the thick of aviation history with competitors using the town as a staging post.

When Western and Provincial Airlines commenced operating in 1935, Narromine had a regular passenger service to Sydney decades before most much larger towns. The town's first hangar (which still stands) was opened in 1937 by the Comptroller of Civil Aviation, Captain Johnson, who said he was sure Narromine would continue to flourish as an aviation centre.

Until this time the airfield had operated mainly through the generosity of Tom Perry, who had also financed the hangar. The

'...the great aviation pioneer, Arthur Butler.' At Narromine 1931.

local council had made numerous appeals to the federal government for grants to ease the burden of philanthropy on Perry, and Captain Johnson became an ally to the cause. It was to take a war, however, before the government came to the aid of this hard working and forward thinking little town.

In April 1940, the Commonwealth acquired the Narromine Aerodrome and set up No. 5 Elementary Flying Training School RAAF. One of the main aims of the aero club, to establish a flying school in the district, had at last been achieved.

During the war over 2000 pilots were trained on Tiger Moths and Wirraways at Narromine. The much extended and improved aerodrome, also home to 618 Squadron, was upgraded to a sufficient standard to be the reserve base for Liberator bombers in the event of Japanese invasion.

When the war ended, some of the original buildings were sold off by the government but, eventually, in 1948, the aero club was again granted use of the ground.

'... the town of Narromine is now a famous centre for aviation heritage'
The Narromine Museum from the air.

Through the 1950s many locals gained their private and commercial flying experience at the aero club. Qantas used the aerodrome as a training centre for over twenty years and it remained under the control of the Commonwealth until Narromine Municipal Council took control in 1975.

Narromine also became a major centre for gliding, when the Dubbo Gliding Club found a new home there and was renamed the Orana Soaring Club in 1975.

That same year the aerodrome once again saw massive crowds when over 5000 people turned out to see the 209 entrants in the New South Wales Air Race land safely. It was reminiscent of those wonderful air pageants of the pre-war period and, before too long, those days were to return.

Through the 1980s and 1990s air shows were once again successfully staged and, in 1988, Narromine was given the honour of being the starting point for the great Bicentennial Air Race around Australia.

The idea of building a museum to tell Narromine's aviation story started to become a reality in the late 1990s, when a committee was formed and a National Tourism Development grant secured. The Narromine Aero Club contributed to the initial collection, and donations of memorabilia were sought.

Narromine Council provided additional funding and a public fundraising effort was hugely successful. The unique museum building, designed with its roof reminiscent of an airfoil, is the result of many years of dreaming and planning, and also some 6000 hours of voluntary labour by Narromine Aero Club members and others.

The Narromine Aviation Museum was officially opened by an old friend of Narromine, Nancy Bird-Walton, in October 2002. The following year Peter Kierath, the museum chairman and son of one of the twelve founder members of the aero club, was pleased to announce that a regional assistance grant had been gained to enable the museum committee to employ an experienced curator.

Mike Nelmes, from the Australian War Memorial, was appointed to the position. As a result of his work and the committee's enthusiasm, displays were developed and practical projects undertaken, including the preservation of the only Hawkridge Venture glider in the world. The wealth of historic material collected over the years was catalogued and sorted, making the museum collection a treasure trove for local historians and researchers.

Narromine Aviation Museum

' ... a very modern museum of aviation history.' Inside the Narromine Aviation Museum.

Narromine is unique in having an unbroken record as a centre of flying excellence and achievement. Many of the people who planned and worked to make the dream of the aviation museum a reality are the sons, daughters, grandsons and granddaughters of the people who first established Narromine's reputation as an aviation centre and a haven of hospitality, help and understanding for so many of our pioneer aviators.

The Wright Flyer replica that took to the air on that October morning in 2005 symbolised Narromine's attitude to aviation heritage. The past was being preserved yet also brought to life. The replica, like the Narromine Aviation Museum and the town itself, is not only a piece of living history and a link to our aviation heritage . . . it actually took off!

Adelaide to Sydney, 1922

Geddes of The Register

Although the aerial mail service between Adelaide and Sydney has been conducted by The Australian Aerial Services Ltd for a period of exactly twelve months without an accident, it has attracted but little attention from the man in the street. Sufficient for him to know that it has carried and delivered the mails every week with commendable regularity. But, as to the why and wherefore, despite the fact that he is contributing to its support, he has little or no interest in it.

Every Saturday morning an aeroplane carrying an air mail bag has left Sydney for Adelaide, and unless something in the way of adverse weather conditions has been experienced, these mail bags have been safely delivered in South Australia's capital the following morning.

Next morning the pilot takes his mails on board, and starts off on his long aerial journey, handing them over to the postal authorities in Sydney the next day. Occasionally he carries one or two passengers, but the desire to rise in the world, at any rate by means of a flying machine, has not yet caught on with the people of Australia. If the service depended for its success on the number of passengers it carried it would have had to close down long ago.

Fortunately, the Federal Government realized that if Australia is ever attacked by an enemy country it will have to depend to a large extent on its air defences, and it is therefore essential to possess an Air Force that can be relied upon to do its part in the event of invasion. To this end it has wisely decided to assist civil aviation as much as possible through postal subsidies and a corps of air pilots who, in time, will come to know practically every mile of Australia. This knowledge would be invaluable in the event of a war.

To obtain his certificate and take charge of an aeroplane a civil air pilot has to be sworn in as a member of the Flying Corps. Out of some 2000 Australians who were engaged in aerial work during the Great War, only about a dozen are following the same pursuit in the Commonwealth today. Most of the pilots in Australia are Englishmen.

Adelaide from the air is very beautiful. The houses look for all the world like those miniature models of villas that are so frequently to be seen in land agents' windows. The mathematical correctness with which the streets are laid out is impressive. The contour of the gulf and the waterways in the neighbourhood of Port Adelaide stand out with extraordinary distinctness, and one realizes what an aid in the mapping out of coastline the aeroplane must be.

The reservoirs to the east of Adelaide shone like large ponds, and a motorcar speeding below appeared about the size of an ordinary thimble.

Crossing the Mount Lofty Range near Mount Pleasant, we took an upward course, and I was impressed with the many beautiful shadow effects on hill and valley. The visibility being good, it was not necessary to rise as high in crossing the ranges as might otherwise have been the case, and it was not long before the Murray came into view.

I was surprised at the quantity of land under cultivation as we crossed the Murray flats, and a remarkable effect was frequently noticeable when passing over a ploughed field, the unploughed edges appearing to stand out in relief as compared with the tilled portion.

We flew over the Murray at Swan Reach at a height of 2000 feet, having covered sixty-eight miles in three-quarters of an hour against a headwind. Trees at this altitude looked like small bushes, and the river appeared about twenty to thirty feet across, and could be seen for miles winding its tortuous course in the direction of Wentworth. On the farther side of the Murray there are large tracts under cultivation, but we were flying at too great a height to discern the houses.

Loxton was sighted; in the distance Lake Victoria could be seen, and there was evidence on all sides of heavy rains having fallen. There was a beautiful kaleidoscopic effect caused by the sun behind the clouds, while the variegated colours of the cultivated sections over which we passed appeared like so many delicate shades of velvet.

At a quarter to three we sighted Wentworth, and I was interested in seeing where the Darling joined the Murray. An artistically laid out soldiers' settlement in the neighbourhood of Wentworth stood out very distinctly, the cultivated area presenting the appearance of a huge billiard table.

Shortly after three o'clock we were over Mildura, and effected a fine landing at the aerodrome, located a mile or two out of the town. Water was observable everywhere; indeed, the whole country appeared to be inundated and miniature lakes could be noticed as far as the eye could see. Although at times we flew low, we met no birds. The only bird life noticeable were flocks of white cockatoos, whose habitat appeared to be in the trees by the side of the river.

We followed the track of the Murray as far as Euston and the next town we sighted was Balranald, on the Murrumbidgee. The country was now absolutely flat, and not a tree could be seen anywhere. We sighted numberless dams, which at the height we were flying appeared to be constructed of cement, and every one was full of water. They seemed no bigger than large saucers.

As we rose higher, the white, fleecy clouds which passed us looked exactly like hundreds of pieces of cotton wool floating through the air. We had now entered the famous Riverina which, I was informed, a week or two before was dry and dusty without a blade of grass for miles. What a wonderful country it is when rain falls. Grass appeared to be springing up everywhere, and the squatters who inhabit this portion of New South Wales are apparently in for a good time.

The Australian Aerial Services Ltd have their workshop at Hay, and employ a skilled staff to keep their aeroplanes in order, overhaul the engines daily and make repairs. It was as well the pilot was thoroughly acquainted with the peculiarities of the aerodrome because, being on a large common, it was underwater in places. He circled two or three times, and eventually made a good landing immediately in front of the hangar. Several of the employees dashed out, kept the plane on the move, and brought it to a stop in a sheltered position.

In view of the reports received from Cootamundra we decided to stay the night at Hay.

I had thought the roads around Mildura in a deplorable condition, but those in and around Hay can only be described as awful. Hay, I believe, was originally called Lang's Crossing, and in the good old days was a most prosperous town. Being in the heart of the Riverina district, it was the rallying point for the squatters of that valuable portion of New South Wales. Its club was conducted on the most correct English lines, and the old inhabitants informed me, speaking of those happy times before strikes and labour troubles had devastated the country, that they remembered powdered footmen, French ladies' maids, and other evidences of old world refinement, gracing the functions of Lang's Crossing in the heyday of its prosperity.

As a casual visitor I should say 'the light of other days has faded'. And when I asked the reason I was told it was the motorcar. Instead of finding their amusements in what I might term their country town, the squatters and their womenfolk jump into their Rolls Royces, speed away to the nearest railway station, and in the course of a few hours are enjoying their cocktails at Menzies or a perfectly served dinner at the Ambassadors.

Hay, I have always been given to understand, in summer is one of the hottest places in Australia; indeed, it used to be a popular saying, west of the Darling, that where heat was concerned there was nothing to compare with 'Hay, Hell and Booligal'. My experience of Hay, however, was that it was extremely cold and, as it depends for its lighting on a few antiquated gas lamps, a stroll through its streets at night is not unattended with danger.

When I expressed my surprise to an old resident, to whom I was introduced, at the absence of electric light and Hay's unmade streets, he informed me that some time ago the government offered the town its choice between electric light and an up-to-date sewerage system, and the ratepayers decided in favour of the latter. I should say they were wise in their choice. Now an enterprising capitalist is coming along with an electric lighting scheme, and Hay will then possess two modern essentials.

With regard to the absence of macadamized roads, the explanation was that there is no stone in or around Hay, and the cost of cartage of good road material is prohibitive. Hay, as most Australians are aware, is located on the Murrumbidgee, and it used to be a standing joke in the town to take a newcomer down to the river, where it is not very wide, and wager drinks with him that he could not throw a stone across the stream. He invariably lost, as it is impossible to find a stone in the neighbourhood. When the joke spread and new chums turned up with stones concealed in their pockets, the 'smart Alecs' of Hay ceased to see any fun in it. It is now only a memory.

Hay possesses one fine residential hotel, Bryants', a reinforced concrete structure designed on modern lines, and possessing its own electric light plant. It is most comfortable. But as Hay has been selected as the central station for The Australian Aerial Services it is certain to become prominent once more.

Pilot Sutcliffe left the aeroplane at Hay, and Pilot Briggs took charge on the trip from Hay to Sydney. Captain Briggs requires no introduction to South Australian readers. His ability as a pilot is known throughout the Commonwealth, and his long residence in Adelaide has caused him to be looked upon as the central state's own.

As far as Narrandera we practically followed the Murrumbidgee and the railway line, and I was impressed with the enormous extent of cultivated land and the huge irrigation schemes that are being carried out. The country looked magnificent, and after the phenomenal rainfall which has fallen in various areas along the Murrumbidgee the land should blossom like the rose. We were able to form an excellent idea of the famous Yanco irrigation scheme, and had a splendid view of Leeton, another extensive irrigation settlement near Narrandera.

The landing place at Narrandera is on the racecourse, but we were advised before leaving Hay that most of it was underwater. Flying low, we saw a motorcar waiting for the mails on a dry spot, so Captain Briggs dropped the bags, and we continued on our way.

We were headed to Cootamundra, two hundred miles from Hay by air, and as we neared this important junction, equidistant from Sydney and Melbourne, all the creeks and rivers were in flood. We were to learn afterwards that the floods in some centres were the highest and most disastrous since the foundation of New South Wales.

We reached 'Coota', as it is locally called, at 9.45 am, and Captain Briggs made a brilliant landing at the local 'drome, which we were glad to find was comparatively dry. We handed over the mails, took on the Sydney bags, had a cup of hot coffee which, like a certain well advertised cocoa, proved 'grateful and comforting,' climbed into our seats again, and in view of the boisterous nature of the weather, prepared for what was likely to prove the worst portion of the journey – the trip over the Great Dividing Range.

We shaped what was practically a direct line for Mittagong, flying over Harden, Gunning, Yass, and Goulburn en route, and following the Sydney–Melbourne railway line at frequent intervals.

Approaching the part of the mountains known as the Cullinan Range, we flew low over the flooded areas, getting an idea of the tremendous rush of water from the hilly country that was the cause of considerable damage. I never realized before in an adequate degree the force of the mountains in the matter of feeding the rivers. The way the rain beat down on the mountains suggested the emptying of thousands of buckets of water on a vast inclined space. Every ledge of rock seemed to be dripping water which, rolling into the valleys below, formed huge streams, ever increasing in volume and strength, and carrying destruction on their way to the sea.

We sighted dozens of homesteads looking like minute islands in a sea of swirling waters. We only saw them for a minute, and could merely conjecture as to their fate. But when I read the next day of the fearful damage wrought by the floods in the area over which we had passed, no one realized more than I did what pygmies we are when opposed to the forces of nature, and how absolutely impotent man is in the face of such stupendous torrents as have their being in mountainous regions like the Great Dividing Range.

Tiring of the unpleasant conditions, Captain Briggs turned the nose of the machine upwards and rose above the low lying clouds. As we emerged from the thick, murky bank we were met with a magnificent sight. As far as the eye could see the Great Dividing Range was covered with white, fleecy clouds, giving it the appearance of a ridge of snow capped mountains. The sun, shining on them in places, provided a scene that was indescribably beautiful.

Between the Great Dividing Range and Sydney are miles of what look like low lying hills, covered with scrub, and as we passed over them they appeared for all the world like the huge dark blue waves one sometimes meets in tropical latitudes.

Nothing I can imagine exceeds the beauty presented from the air by Sydney and the contiguous coastline. I have a distinct remembrance of a certain spring morning when, having crossed the Swiss Alps, I left Domo d'Ossala in a snowstorm on my way to Milan. Suddenly the sun blazed out, revealing the Italian lakes – Como, Lugano, and Maggiore – in all their marvellous beauty, and furnishing an entrancing view of the plains of Lombardy and the picturesque towns and villages scattered over them. I have seen many wonderful sights in my lifetime, but they must all take a back seat to Sydney as viewed from the air.

Fringed by the blue Pacific, the picturesque South Coast could be seen as far, I should say, as Jervis Bay, while Broken Bay and the Hawkesbury were clearly visible to the north. As we headed for the aerodrome, which is located at Mascot, near Botany, we had a magnificent view of the national park, Port Hacking, and the Hacking River, while Cronulla beach stood out in all its beauty. Having feasted our eyes on the glories of Botany Bay, George's River, and other well known landmarks in the vicinity, Captain Briggs headed for Port Jackson and flew over the harbour, making a turn just over Circular Quay.

The dozens of ferry boats, huge oceanliners, yachts, and sailing craft of all descriptions, made a never-to-be-forgotten picture, and the harbour, with its numberless little bays and thousands of red-tiled villas running down to the water's edge, presented a veritable fairy scene. The Parramatta River, stretching away like a streak of silver in the distance, added to the beauty of the *tout ensemble*, and as I gazed on the exquisite vision I had to allow that Sydney people have every justification for being proud of their peerless harbour.

A beautiful landing at 12.40 pm and twenty minutes later we were doing justice to a dainty lunch in a Sydney club with appetites sharpened by our dash, at nearly a hundred miles an hour, through the keen mountain air at an altitude of about 4000 feet.

A Bird has to Fly

Jillian Dellit

Nancy Bird was born in Kew, on the New South Wales north
coast, in 1915, a year all Australians recognise as the year of
the Gallipoli landing.

Later in her life, however, Nancy marked 1915 as the year that
the Australian military became airborne, in response to a request
from the Indian government for air support in the Middle East.
She also noted that, at the time, the Australian military flying
school had two aeroplanes and a box kite.

As the aviation industry in Australia developed through its
childhood and adolescence to maturity, so did Nancy Bird.

Most of Nancy's contemporaries were content to wait for the
benefits the new form of transport would bring to them. She,
however, chose to put her energy behind the fledgling industry,
helping it to gain momentum. Her life mirrors aviation's struggle
and achievement in Australia.

By the time Nancy was four, Billy Hughes, with his interest in
aviation, was prime minister and her imagination was fuelled by
media stories of aviators as they pioneered the England to Australia
and USA to Australia air routes. Hughes understood the potential

of aviation to connect Australia to European markets and his government looked for ways to encourage the expansion of air links.

Nancy's whole family moved to Collaroy, then Dee Why and finally Manly. Just before the Depression her father bought a business on the Manning River at Mt George and Nancy was taken out of school, two months before her fourteenth birthday, to be his housekeeper and bookkeeper.

The Depression made life harder for everyone and its impact was felt in every part of Australia. The books Nancy kept told of deprivation, long term debt and hard times. The steady stream of itinerants needing sustenance told a further story of insecurity and poverty.

A few enterprising ex-servicemen were trying to feed their families and their thirst for flying by putting on air pageants in large country towns. On race or show day, go-ahead country towns would clear a paddock next to the racecourse or showground for any pilot who would come and offer joyrides.

Pilots soon learned that they could plot a circuit around the country following the races and shows. 'Barnstorming' kept them in the air and at least paid for petrol and maintenance. Pilots who could purchase, borrow or hire a plane would descend on a country town and entertain locals with aerobatics, signwriting and flypasts before selling five minute joyrides. It was a hazardous way of making a living, given the costs of petrol and maintenance, and especially so in the Depression when few people had money for luxuries and extras.

Nancy's father paid her £1 a week. On her half day a week off, she managed to get into Wingham on an air pageant day and took a joyride. She then took a second flight and conned the pilot into doing aerobatics for an extra £1.

She got herself a copy of *Learning to Fly* by Frank Swoffer. It didn't turn her into a pilot, but it fuelled her ambition, confirmed her commitment and increased her saving zeal. By the age of fifteen she had enough money to take a trial instructional flight while in Sydney visiting her mother.

Every new step she took was towards her goal and every step strengthened her ambition. At the end of that flight she had enough money left to buy a helmet . . . although she had to ask the instructor where to buy it.

She took inspiration from flyers like Amy Johnson and, when the German aviatrix Elly Beinhorn visited Sydney in 1932 to promote her book, Nancy made sure she was in Grace Bros department store to see her.

When another barnstormer came to Wingham the next year, with two aircraft, Nancy hoped to have a lesson, but had to be content with a flight. She talked to the pilot of the larger aircraft who told her he was opening a flying school. He said to her, 'Why don't you come to Sydney and we'll teach you to fly?' His name was Charles Kingsford Smith.

So, on 11 August 1933, Nancy turned up at Mascot to be one of Smithy's first pupils.

By 1933 she had saved £200. So at seventeen she defied her father and moved to the family home at Manly. The other children could take their turn at supporting the family store. Nancy was learning to fly.

The Depression was ending. Governments were seeking ways to link Australia more effectively to Europe, and everywhere ordinary people wanted their lives to improve.

There were a few people, both men and women, with sufficient money and enthusiasm to learn to fly for sport. They created a small demand for flying instruction and opportunities to fly. Thanks to the persistence of a few World War I veterans, Australia had a small network of experienced, mostly male, pilots who were trying to make a living by meeting this demand, hoping to develop an aviation industry. Nancy was joining this network.

Every day she caught the ferry to Circular Quay, got the Botany tram to Mascot and walked the mile from the post office tram stop to the airport. When Kingsford Smith was in Sydney he might pick her up from the Manly ferry at Circular Quay and drive her the rest of the way. He didn't approve of women flying, but he knew that they paid good money and being short of cash, was only too happy to have paying pupils. Much of his time, however, was spent away, attempting long distance records or pursuing charter work.

He had set up his flying school in a hangar that housed the *Southern Cross* at Mascot. From here he gave Nancy her first two lessons before he again headed overseas and Pat Hall, Smithy's chief instructor, took over the job.

Nancy ignored the views about women flyers held by most of the men in the hangar. When she asked to learn engineering she was given the dirtiest jobs to put her off . . . and she ignored that too. She took the lessons, listened to the talk in the hangar and at the aero club, watched others fly, and went up with anyone who would take her.

Many fellow students were wealthy, flying for sport or to be daring. Jobs were scarce in aviation. The dream of reducing time and distance was tantalising, but making flying affordable was a challenge.

Any job that kept planes in the air and pilots in work was important. Although businesses could see possibilities in using aviation, initially they were cautious and held back by costs. For example, newspapers grasped the advantage of merging the new photographic technology with flight. For special events such as royal visits or the Melbourne Cup they chartered planes to get stories and photos to press, but they didn't do this for daily reporting. Air mail routes were beginning to develop although they weren't all regular. Sydney-Brisbane was successful but Melbourne-Sydney failed after the loss of the *Southern Cloud*, which sent Smithy and Ulm into liquidation.

The prizes offered by State governments in air races to their cities were important incentives and, around the fringes, pilots scraped a living from charter work and air pageants.

The Dutch had services from Holland to Java and the British from London to Singapore. Both advertised for tenders for an Australian extension of their service. Qantas won the Singapore tender against a bid from Kingsford Smith, Ulm and others.

In 1934, while still a student, Nancy teamed with a New Zealander, Jean Batten, to offer joyrides at the Cootamundra Air Pageant. In the same year Jean Batten was the commentator for the MacRobertson air race. Jean held the England to Australia record for a woman and, in 1935, she set the world record for any plane flying from England to Brazil. In 1936, against all advice, she successfully flew solo from England to Auckland.

Although the opportunities, records and events kept would-be pilots motivated, there was plenty to discourage them. Many early aviation companies went into liquidation. Crashes were so routine that students checked for them every morning around the periphery of the aerodrome at Mascot. In those years it was not unusual for planes, and the bodies of their occupants, to be dragged from Botany Bay and the Georges River.

None of this discouraged Nancy Bird. In 1935, at the age of nineteen, she had a licence to 'fly for hire or reward' and had to make her own way. No one was going to give her a job; to sell her services she needed a plane . . . and she had no money.

National Library of Australia (nla.pic-vn3302813): Nancy Bird-Walton and her Gipsy Moth plane.

' ... at the age of 19, she had a licence to 'fly for hire or reward'.

But flying was what she had to do. A great aunt offered to give her £200 instead of money in her will and she went to her father for another £200 to enable her to keep flying. With this money she bought a Gipsy Moth aircraft from the estate of the late Reg Annabel. Reg was the pilot who had taken her up on her first flight, as a fifteen-year-old, at the Wingham air show. Reg had rebuilt the Gipsy Moth from a wreck. He had been killed in an aerobatic accident over Mascot.

Nancy then asked Peg MacKillop from her flying class to go barnstorming with her. Peg wanted to fly, had independent means and didn't need to be paid. Armed with an agreement to use Shell petrol and a list of country shows and races obtained from a newspaper, they set off for Tamworth and billed themselves as the 'First Ladies' Flying Tour'.

Tamworth had an aero club with no planes and a gliding club with one crashed glider; the mayor gave the 'First Ladies' a civic reception. It was there in Tamworth that Eric Baume of Sydney radio fame paid them £10 to write 'Woman' under the wings of their plane, in order to advertise the new women's magazine of that name.

Inverell was their second stop. It was the first race day after fourteen years of drought, and a local farmer paid for all the kids to be taken up for joyrides.

On their two barnstorming tours the ladies dealt with all their own mechanical troubles and often had problems starting the engines. A tyre they blew had to be replaced from Sydney because there was no local supply.

It was an expensive and unreliable business, but they were independent and they were getting plenty of customers. Even if they were just paying the bills and scraping along, they were making plenty of friends in the towns and on the outback stations.

Many of those they met were looking for new ways of improving the lives and opportunities of those who lived in the country. Nancy knew aviation could help.

In Narromine they met Tom Perry, who had given land for an aerodrome and financed Western and Southern Airlines. He chartered the Gipsy Moth to inspect land at Dubbo. He gave Nancy a lot of encouragement, along with the idea of getting a larger plane.

At Dubbo she had met Stanley Drummond, founder of the Far West Children's Health Scheme. Since 1924 he had been bringing children with trachoma to Sydney for treatment and organising city holidays for country kids. He had recently begun taking children's health clinics to the far west in railway carriages, which were shunted to sidings to serve as local clinics. He was trying to send nurses by car to those families who lived beyond the reach of the railways. Drummond saw the potential for improving these services and saving time by flying the nurses to distant stations, and he offered Nancy the opportunity to trial a flight service from Bourke.

The ladies fitted this trial in between their two hectic barnstorming tours and winning second prize in the Closed Circuit Aerial Derby at the Narromine Air Pageant of 1935.

So, on her twentieth birthday, Nancy Bird was working an air charter for the Far West Children's Health Scheme, ferrying Sister Webb to homes beyond Burke for basic preventative medicine clinics, playing her part in influencing a new generation of mothers away from the bread and dripping survival techniques of the Depression. Landing in rough, uncharted paddocks around the junction of New South Wales, Queensland and South Australia, and with a road as the only landmark for flying, they took the service to places where fruit and vegetables were luxuries and women regularly died in childbirth.

Flight was making a difference; it was helping to reduce ignorance and isolation, improving the health of outback women and children – and saving lives.

The trial ended in an offer of a contract. Stanley Drummond would contract Nancy Bird for six months on a £100 retainer with a guarantee of another £100 work. Stationed in Bourke, she was free to supplement this income with charter work.

Nancy immediately sold the Gipsy Moth and went into debt to buy a £1700 Leopard Moth, which doubled her carrying capacity . . . from one to two passengers. At twenty years of age she had become the first woman to own and operate a commercial air service in Australia. More importantly she had the courage to try to make a living providing a service that changed lives.

For three years she pioneered services to outback stations, first from Bourke and then from Charleville and Cunnamulla. She wore practical clothes, mostly hand-me-downs from her sisters, and a pith helmet to keep cool in summer.

In addition to transporting nurses to clinics, she acted as an aerial ambulance, organised Father Christmas for outback kids, and took stock agents to visit properties when the drought broke. She either performed her own maintenance or engaged the services of the auto engineer in Bourke and the shire engineer in Cunnamulla.

When she got lost she landed at homesteads and asked the way.

In their pioneering journey from England to Australia, Keith and Ross Smith had had the services of 200 convicts in Surabaya to clear tree stumps from an airfield. Nancy had station hands or families hastily take down fences and she asked women to spread sheets over the worst stumps and holes. She navigated with a compass, her watch and a ruler, using landmarks such as dead horses, fresh droppings or the 'dog fence'. She had no landing instruments, no lights for night flying, no radio and little if any backup. No service tracked her whereabouts and her plane was frequently overloaded to get the job done.

On short notice she went wherever the work took her. It might be local, it might be Adelaide. Often, in bad weather, she would fly just above the treetops following the fences, railway lines, rivers, or landmarks that became known to her. Sometimes she would chase a train to overtake it for a client.

There are people today who remember helping to load or unload the sick from her plane and there are also some who owe their lives to her service.

Although a determined doctor in Darwin had become a 'flying doctor' in the mid-1920s, and the Australian Inland Mission had established its Flying Doctor bases in Cloncurry and Broken Hill by the mid-1930s, there were still very few inland medical services in 1936. Nancy's work was pioneering and remarkable.

In 1936 she entered the South Australian government's air race from Brisbane to Adelaide via Sydney and Melbourne. The race was won by a Victorian, Hamilton garage owner, Reg Ansett. Flying solo, Nancy won the Ladies' Trophy and set the record between Melbourne and Adelaide. This experience brought her back into the company of other aviators, including Jean Batten and four other women competitors. Although it reduced her feelings of loneliness, it also highlighted her isolation.

In the same year, the Commonwealth government withdrew its subsidy for the Far West Children's Health Scheme. With no need to stay in Bourke, and in need of replacement business and better aviation support, Nancy moved her base to Charleville and tried convincing the Queensland government to set up a similar far west scheme.

Charleville was the lunch stop on the Qantas route from Sydney to Singapore and it had an aeronautical engineer. The engineering and hangar costs however, proved too expensive for Nancy and the Queensland government rejected her idea.

She moved again in 1937, this time to Cunnamulla. Many of her customers remained loyal and moved with her, so she was often doing long flights, starting early to beat the heat. Amelia Earhart came to Australia in that year, landing in Darwin. Nancy wanted to fly to meet her, but couldn't afford the petrol from Cunnamulla. From Darwin, Amelia went on to New Guinea and was subsequently lost over the Pacific.

It was not just the three years of flying alone in hard conditions that took their toll and led to Nancy's decision to give up flying in 1937. In what might today be termed 'burn out' she also seems to have been worn down by the negative messages of influential people and the fact that she never had enough money to do what she knew was needed.

Smithy, the aviator she most admired, had seen no place for women in the industry, governments were slow and unreliable in subsidising medical and social services to the far west, and even John Flynn, whom she respected, had begged her to give up when he passed through Cunnamulla, telling her that the work was too much for a woman.

At the end of a trip to Sydney she called it quits ... for the time being.

Before long, Nancy had another idea.

Journalists had written about her in newspapers and women's magazines, so her name and story were well known. This led KPM, the Dutch shipping company with airline interests, to invite her to be their guest on one of the first Royal Netherland Indies (KLM) flights from Australia to Java, connecting with their onward service to Europe.

Nancy, always looking for other possibilities in the aviation industry, saw this as an opportunity to study ground organisation in Europe.

First, however, she went, as part of a delegation from the National Council of Women, to see the prime minister, Joe Lyons, in a last ditch attempt to have the Far West Children's subsidy reinstated. When this failed she accepted the KPM invitation.

She told the *Sydney Morning Herald*:

> I will concentrate on the study of commercial ground organization from the passenger's point of view. If possible I want to obtain a job at some of the airports in Holland, England and America, to learn first-hand everything I can – about passenger and traffic management in civil aviation.

It was a far-sighted decision. In The Hague, seeing her publicity value, KLM organised free travel for her throughout Europe. Nancy provided articles for the *Sydney Morning Herald*. She travelled on the new KLM Amsterdam to Manchester route and gave the company even more good publicity. She broadcast for the BBC.

In thirteen months she traveled 45 000 miles and visited twenty-five countries. She met Lord Wakefield, who had provided Amy Johnson's fuel, and she was received at Buckingham Palace.

Nancy's later accounts of this event suggest she was underestimated by the Australian social set at Buckingham Palace that day. On the other hand, many influential, enterprising and in some cases wealthy, aviation industry leaders of Europe recognised a kindred spirit and she felt at home in their company. They shared her vision and commitment. She was drawn to the Dutch and German experiences; the British, she felt, were far slower than the Dutch to understand the possibilities of aviation.

Nancy took German lessons so that she could converse with the leading German pilots. She met Albert Plesman, the founder of KLM, and other greats of the aviation industry. She formed a lasting friendship with Elly Beinhorn whom she had met at that book signing in Sydney all those years before. She even flew to the 1938 Paris Air Show as Elly's navigator in a Messerschmitt 108. She also flew with Alex Henshaw, the greatest Spitfire pilot of them all.

As she travelled she collected many items, including models of planes not yet seen in Australia, for an exhibition on aviation she planned to stage when she returned to her homeland.

She finished her travels in the United States where she met women from the 'Ninety Nines' – the Women Pilots' Association of the United States. She joined the organisation as an overseas member and learned about their annual 'Powder Puff Derby'. She then flew to Washington in the newly released DC-9.

In 1939 Nancy returned to Australia by ship. It was on this voyage that she met her future husband, Charles Walton. They were married in Sydney by the Reverend John Flynn in August 1939, after her Aviation Exhibition had been successfully staged in both Sydney and Melbourne.

Nancy Bird had done remarkable things. From struggling to provide a regional pioneering service in outback Australia she had made the leap to understanding how the whole industry might work across the world in the future.

When she had been flattened, exhausted and discouraged, she had widened her horizons and set out to learn more, taking an industry view of aviation.

With her wide knowledge and deep experience she was able to contribute to the development of the Australian Women's Flying Club as it went on to a war footing, training its members in aircraft maintenance, navigation and meteorology.

In 1940 each State formed a branch of the Women's Air Training Corps and, in 1941, the Women's Australian Auxiliary Air Force was authorised by the Commonwealth government. Nancy Bird was commandant of the New South Wales Women's Air Training Corps throughout the war. She, along with other female aviators, remained doggedly critical of the Australian government's failure to follow the lead of the British and US governments and use women to ferry planes to where they were needed as part of the war effort.

After the war she took a few years off to raise her family, but remained active in community life, even going to the far west as a dental nurse with the Far West Children's Health Scheme in 1950.

Nancy took out a student pilot licence in 1951, which enabled her to fly as co-pilot to her friend Mae Casey, something she continued to do even after Mae's husband became Governor-General in 1965.

She maintained links with her friends around the world, including her German friends, many of whom she visited after the war. In 1958 she renewed her full pilot's licence for a trip to the USA. As she would be there for the American All Women's Transcontinental Air Race, the 'Powder Puff Derby', she filled out the forms before she even had a sponsor, plane or co-pilot. Hers was the first ever overseas entry and her gamble, of course, paid off. She hired a Cessna 172 and learned to fly it while friends in the States found her a co-pilot. They came fifth and won $200.

Nancy flew in three more Powder Puff Derbies. In 1966 she was the only original competitor to fly in a re-enactment of the 1936 Brisbane to Adelaide race. She also flew with Dick and Ian Smith in the Perth to Sydney air race in the early 1970s.

Her commitment to making sure the benefits of aviation reached the whole community has continued throughout her long life. She has maintained her links with the international network of women pilots and supported Australian women who wanted to fly. A relentless advocate for aerial services for rural communities, she has told the stories of Australian aviation – the pioneers, the

Nancy Bird-Walton ' … she took as much interest in the people around her as she did in the aeronautics.'

women and the communities – in books, talks, interviews, articles and films.

In 2000 Nancy was on board the 747 round trip flight from Sydney to Wollongong to celebrate Sydney Airport Corporation's eightieth anniversary. Accounts of the event note that she took as much interest in the people around her as she did in the aeronautics.

She was present on 18 July 2005, at the launch of *Sydney Airport: 85 Years as the Gateway to Australia*, a book celebrating Sydney Airport's anniversary and, on 16 October 2005, at her ninetieth birthday dinner, Qantas announced that its first A380 aircraft was to be called 'Nancy Bird-Walton'.

EDITORS' NOTE: There is more information about Nancy Bird-Walton AO, OBE, Hon. DSc., Hon. ME on the websites of the Australian Women Pilots' Association, the National Library of Australia, the *Dictionary of Australian Biography*, the ABC, the Australian Aviation Museum Bankstown, and the *Sydney Morning Herald*. Nancy has written two autobiographies, *Born to Fly* and *My God, It's a Woman*. This story owes much to these sources.

The Royal Flying Doctor Service

Jim Haynes

One of Australia's most loved institutions is the Royal Flying Doctor Service (RFDS). In rural areas of Australia fundraising continues from year to year and outback folk never refuse an invitation to buy a raffle ticket or attend a function if the money is for the RFDS.

On 15 May 1928 the Aerial Medical Service was established as a one year experiment at Cloncurry, Queensland, by the Reverend John Flynn, head of the Australian Inland Mission, a Presbyterian Church initiative. The service survived the Great Depression of the late 1920s and early 1930s and, by 1932, the AIM had a network of ten little hospitals across the centre. The service continued to grow over the next few years.

Although the service suffered severe financial difficulties, its continuing success at Cloncurry caught the imagination of people around the country and the world, and prompting John Flynn and Dr Alan Vickers to push for a network of flying doctor bases spread across the continent, with government support.

In 1934 the Presbyterian Church handed the service over to the Australian Aerial Medical Service. Over the next few years, sections were established across Australia with their operational bases at Wyndham, Port Hedland, Kalgoorlie, Broken Hill, Alice Springs and Meekatharra, along with two additional Queensland bases at Charters Towers and Charleville.

In 1936 a coordinating Federal Council was created. In 1942 the service was renamed the Flying Doctor Service and use of the Royal prefix was granted in 1955.

The Flying Doctor

C. J. Dennis

They sang of old when the land was young
Of many a bushman's feat;
In many a hut has the song been sung
Of a leg across the saddle flung
And the lilt of a galloping beat.

As Jack or Bill with teeth set tight,
And never a pause for breath,
Went galloping, galloping into the night,
Summoning aid to the parlous plight
Of a good mate, sick to death.

But who shall sing of a newer thing,
Of the flying medico?
High aloft on a rushing wing,
Speeding on, swift hope to bring
To the lonely folk below.

And who shall sing of a lonely land,
That is lonely nevermore,
Since man has schemed, and man has planned
Time defeated, distance spanned,
Where the flying doctors soar?

They sang of old of a long, long tramp
Thro' the miles of bush forlorn,
Into a town from a distant camp,
Hoping still while the flickering lamp
Burned low in the burden borne:

They sang of the labour bushmen gave
For the sake of a stricken friend,
Seeking grimly a life to save;
And a needless death and a lonely grave
Was the sum of all, in the end.

But who shall sing of the soaring wing,
And the help that comes from high?
Of the flying doctor who shall sing
Rushing to aid a stricken thing,
Out of a bushland sky?

And who shall sing of the swift replies
To the call of a message drear,
Of the quickened hope and the anxious eyes
Gazing into the empty skies,
And the gladsome shout, 'He's here!'

'Out of a bushland sky ...' Flying Doctor over Central Australia.

Birth of an Airline

Jim Haynes

When World War I flying aces Paul McGinness and Hudson Fysh were given a job scouting out a route and constructing airstrips for the 1919 London to Sydney Air Race, they came into first hand contact with the difficulties of getting around in the bush.

Fysh and McGinness were both Gallipoli veterans. McGinness won a Distinguished Conduct Medal for bravery at Gallipoli and he and Fysh met there and later both transferred to No 1 Squadron Australian Flying Corps, trained as airmen, and flew in the Middle East.

One hot Sunday afternoon in Cloncurry, driving to a picnic, McGinness met influential grazier, Fergus McMaster, one of the founders of the Country Party in Queensland.

McMaster's car had broken an axle in the dusty bed of the Cloncurry River and he had walked to town for a replacement. The garage was closed, perhaps its owner was at the picnic, so McGinness cheerfully removed corrugated iron from the garage wall and found an axle.

He drove McMaster back to his car and helped the older man fix it.

The seeds of a future partnership were planted and, as a result, on 20 June 1920, McGinness and Fysh sat with McMaster at a glass topped table in Brisbane's elegant Gresham Hotel to register a new airline company. Alan Campbell of Queensland Primary Producers sat in as adviser.

Still young, still feeling displaced by their war experience and too restless for ordinary occupations, McGinness and Fysh were determined to seize their chance.

They tried a number of different names for the company and finally one was chosen; Queensland And Northern Territory Aerial Services Limited, QANTAS.

McMaster would become QANTAS' most formidable powerbroker. He lobbied his fellow graziers and ex-army friends to invest in QANTAS and, after McGinness had talked to Prime Minister Billy Hughes, McMaster helped broker a deal for a federal government subsidy for QANTAS by trading off Country Party support for the Government Estimates Bill to pass through parliament. It was also Fergus McMaster who insisted upon a total alcohol ban for QANTAS pilots in the early days. He remained as chairman until his retirement in 1947.

Fysh also remained a part of QANTAS all his life and both he and McMaster were knighted for their services to Australian Aviation. McGinness moved on after a few years (he was never happy with the total alcohol ban) and pursued various business ventures in Western Australia. He returned east to train pilots at Point Cook in World War II.

QANTAS was incorporated in November of 1920 and the first board meeting was held at Winton, in the Winton Club which is still there today. It was the only meeting held in Winton, as a decision was promptly taken to shift company headquarters to Longreach. It was more prudent to be closer to the railhead, with easier access for passengers and spare parts.

On 21 May 1921, the first annual general meeting of shareholders was held at Longreach. The principal backers in hard cash were Ainslie Templeton, McGinness, McMaster, Fysh, and

Longreach doctor, F. A. Hope Michod. The original paid-up capital was six thousand, eight hundred and fifty pounds.

The rest is history.

'The rest is history ...' Hudson Fysh and two passengers with first Qantas aerial mail service about to depart Charleville, Queensland, 2nd November 1922.

The Aussie Airline

Jim Haynes

There's a hangar out at Longreach, a relic of the past,
That was first home to an airline that, it seems, was built to last.
An airline that was born upon a hot November day
In the year of 1920 and went on to show the way
To every other airline that you just might care to name,
The second oldest in the world, that's just one claim to fame.
The oldest airline anywhere they use the English tongue,
And the safest airline ever, though born when flight was young.
Born out of a necessity, in this great land of ours,
To lessen isolation, turn weeks and months to hours,
To join the city to the bush, to keep the flag unfurled,
And go on to join our isolated nation to the world.
Its symbol is an icon, the flying kangaroo,
It shows what good old Aussie ingenuity can do.
I'm sure Sir Hudson would be proud, that famous flying Fysh,
To see it flying safely still; so here's a final wish;
May QANTAS and the flying kangaroo fly on forever,
And safely bring the whole world, and Australians, together.

Qantas Founders' Outback Museum, Longreach

'There's a hangar out at Longreach ...'

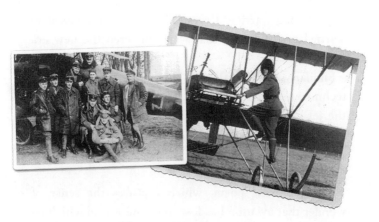

PART 2

'MOST CONSPICUOUS BRAVERY' – WAR IN THE AIR

Powered flight was just a decade into its development when World War I began. The new technology was always going to be adapted to killing and the Great War merely hastened the process.

The first roles for aircraft in war were reconnaissance and observation, but bombs and guns were soon being deployed from aircraft and the first aircraft to aircraft fatality occurred on 5 October 1914 when a French observer in a Voisin shot a German Aviatik scout over Rheims.

As is normal in wartime the development of new technology accelerated, exacting an awful death toll from among wartime flyers. The surviving pilots who learned to fly during that war pioneered the new era of aviation.

Similarly World War II heralded a new age of technology in flying and accelerated the development of the jet engine. This enabled the breakthroughs of the postwar era that eventually led to the passenger services and regular everyday world of aviation that we enjoy today.

The following poem, which captures the sense of wonder that aviation has lost since the war in which its author died, is a perfect preface to this sad collection of wartime stories.

High Flight

John Magee

(Killed in a Spitfire over England, 1941, aged nineteen)

Oh! I have slipped the surly bonds of earth
And danced the skies on laughter-silvered wings;
Sunward I've climbed, and joined the tumbling mirth
Of sun-split clouds – and done a hundred things
You have not dreamed of – wheeled and soared and swung
High in the sunlit silence. Hov'ring there,
I've chased the shouting wind along, and flung
My eager craft through footless halls of air.
Up, up the long, delirious, burning blue
I've topped the wind-swept heights with easy grace
Where never lark, or even eagle flew –
And, while with silent lifting mind I've trod
The high untrespassed sanctity of space,
Put out my hand and touched the face of God.

War and Circuses

Charles Kingsford Smith

There comes a time in the lives of most young men when they have to make decisions – I mean decisions which will affect the future course of their lives.

Some of us are born to the humdrum, placid existence of city life; some are born wanderers; others are impatient of the yoke and are a law unto themselves, and some are content to drift along in the path that leads nowhere.

I do not know in which category to place myself. I think perhaps that my future was determined on that day in 1915, my eighteenth birthday, when I presented myself at the recruiting office in Sydney Town Hall and enlisted in the Signal Engineers AIF.

Not that there was anything special about that. Everyone was joining up in those hectic days, but from that hall in Australia to France and England in wartime was a short cut. That, in itself, meant a violent change in one's life.

Until then, I had been an Australian schoolboy, 'messing about' with electric gadgets and interested in engines of all kinds, and consequently apprenticed by my parents to the electrical engineering trade.

Most men look back to their war days with disgust and horror. So do I, but I must confess that I didn't dislike it at the time. The war meant to me a change of scene, a plunge into a big adventure, a new life, new countries. But first there were early days of training as a soldier in the Australian army, in my first unit, the 19th Battery AIF. Somehow or other, guns did not appeal to me, so I got a transfer to the signal corps, and it was with the signallers that I found myself in Egypt and thereafter in Gallipoli, where we remained until the evacuation.

That was certainly an exciting enough adventure for most of us who were still in our teens, but it was hardly the sort of adventure we had visualised in our hot young dreams.

From Gallipoli to France via Egypt was but a step, a step that led to another change for me, from the signal corps to the motorcycle despatch riders, a more interesting occupation for one whose thoughts were largely centred on speed, and on gadgets devised to produce it.

I might have been a despatch rider for the 'duration'; returning when demobbed to Australia, like many thousands of my cobbers, to the humdrum life of peace. But there came a day in 1916 when an opportunity offered itself to become, if not an airman, at least to have the chance of training for a commission in the then Royal Flying Corps.

'It was the chance of a lifetime.'
Recruitment poster for RAF,
late in WW1.

It was the chance of a lifetime; it proved to be the chance of my flying life, and it was a decision I made without a moment's hesitation. I was not peculiar in this respect. There were hundreds, thousands situated like me, each of whom would have given their soul cases to have been selected for the RFC. But although many were called, few were chosen, and those of us who were selected left for our new life, envied by our fellow diggers whom we left behind.

The story of the 'War Birds' over France in those hectic days of 1917 and 1918 has been told by many. I will not linger over them myself, except to remark, in passing, that they were great days. There were giants in the sky then — Albert Ball, Jimmy McCudden, Mannock, Bishop and the Frenchmen Nungesser, Guynemer, Garros and others.

And on 'the other side' there were foemen worthy of our steel, and of our Lewis Vickers guns; such as Immelmann of 'The Turn',

BE2   BE8

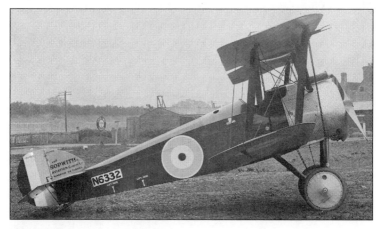

Sopwith Camel

'The famous French 'Spads' ... with which my own squadron, the 23rd, was equipped.'

the slickest and quickest method of doubling in one's track, Richthofen and his circus and others.

The names of these great fighting pilots stand out, but there are hundreds of others of equal calibre whose names are unknown except to their own comrades and to those in their immediate circle who knew of their deeds, and their exploits with the flying gun.

And the machines we flew!

The old names recur to me like wraiths from the past. Maurice Farman, the BE's, the Martinsydes, the DH2, Camels and Pups, the wonderful SE5, noted for its speed, and last but not least, the machines with which my own squadron, the 23rd, was equipped – the famous French 'Spads'.* And on 'the other side', the Rumplers, Albatross and Fokkers, whose machine guns were timed to fire ahead through the propellers.

Queer old antediluvian craft they seem now, looking back across the years, but what tricks we performed in them, what feats of daring were accomplished.

I came into the world of flying at its dawn, and what a glorious dawn! There was barely a glimpse of dawn in those dark drear days of 1914 when the sole idea in air warfare was that the machines were designed, and the men were trained, for reconnaissance only.

They were to be scouts, the eyes of the army. But long before Armistice Day arrived, the flying forces of all the combatants had

*EDITORS' NOTE: 'Spads' were built by the 'Societe Pour Aviation et ses Derives', a firm founded by M. Bleriot, the famous airman who was the first to fly across the English Channel.

'I came into the world of flying at its dawn ...' Charles Kingsford Smith.

reached a pitch of development in design, speed, fighting power which, two years earlier, had hardly been dreamt of.

Everything was in a state of flux, so rapid were the developments taking place almost from day to day. And among the pilots was a keen and friendly rivalry to outdo each other, which nothing could dampen.

When we were not dodging the German 'Archies' we were on patrol, or loosing off drums of Lewis or Vickers bullets, or engaged in performing terrific stunts in fighting aviation known as the 'zoom' or the 'roll', or the 'dive.'

Our planes flew and fought at 15 000 feet, a tremendous ceiling in those days; the Spads had a top speed even then (and that was nearly twenty years ago) of 130 mph and a ceiling of 20 000 feet.

Sometimes our squadrons would sweep the sky in bands twenty strong, looking for trouble in the shape of the Hun machines, and generally finding it. We flew low over enemy aerodromes and trenches, ground strafing and attacking anything in sight with our drums of Lewis fire.

At other times we flew high, waiting at 15 000 feet to pounce on our enemies, and there were exciting and adventurous occasions when we deliberately cultivated a spinning nosedive in an effort to avoid attack, or with nonchalant abandon rolled carefree.

But, underneath this youthful impetuosity and superficial gaiety, there was a deadly concentration of purpose and superb nervous stability. You hardly ever heard of an airman having a nervous breakdown in those days, though how we managed to avoid them with all that immense output of energy, I do not know.

I expect it was just youth living on its nerves. Another memory of those days comes to me – of the long summer evenings of 1918 over the famous old Salient; there is, too, still in my nostrils the unmistakable odour of the German tracer bullets as they streamed past like a jet from a hose, and I recall the joy of battle when one first 'bagged one's own bird' and had the inexpressible relief of seeing the enemy going down to disaster.

Julian Grenfell, in his poem 'Into Battle', expressed the thoughts of the fighting airmen of the Western Front, though he died not knowing of the tremendous developments that were to take place in the air.

> The naked earth is warm with spring,
> And with green grass and bursting trees
> Leans to the sun's gaze glorying,
> And quivers in the sunny breeze;
> And life is colour and warmth and light,
> And a striving evermore for these;
> And he is dead who will not fight;
> And who dies fighting has increase.
>
> The fighting man shall from the sun
> Take warmth, and life from the glowing earth;
> Speed with the light-foot winds to run,
> And with the trees to newer birth;
> And find, when fighting shall be done,
> Great rest, and fullness after dearth. . . .
>
> And when the burning moment breaks,
> And all things else are out of mind,

And only joy of battle takes
Him by the throat, and makes him blind,

Through joy and blindness he shall know
Not caring much to know, that still
Nor lead nor steel shall reach him, so
That it be not the Destined Will.

The thundering line of battle stands,
And in the air death moans and sings;
But Day shall clasp him with strong hands,
And Night shall fold him in soft wings.

But why linger over those hectic days on the Western Front? In our funny old machines, prodigious feats were performed by 'intrepid airmen' in things tied up with bits of string, and when it was not unknown for the *London Gazette* to announce that a packet of Military Crosses had been handed out to as many young subalterns and airmen for 'distinguished service'.

I managed to shoot down a few 'Huns', as we called them in those good old days, and I managed to get wounded and shot down myself. It was service all right, though I doubt whether it was very distinguished, but all the time we were youngsters learning a lot. We were imbibing an immense store of flying experience and technical knowledge, and we were learning something which to my mind is far more valuable – the capacity to look after yourself, the instinct to do or to die, the desire for action, without thought of the risks and dangers.

For one thing, you had to be wounded, and I duly received my 'Blighty', a fact which enabled me to take further and more advanced courses in flying, with the result that by the summer of 1918, when I was barely twenty-one, I became an instructor.

It might seem a little presumptuous to many people that a youth not yet twenty-one should take upon himself the style, title and dignity of 'instructor RAF'.

The truth was that I, and many more like me, felt in those days that we could instruct anybody in anything. We thought we knew everything, from how to win the war down to the stripping and re-assembly of any aero engine you liked to place in front of us.

We were a carefree, cigarette smoking, leave seeking lot of young devils who feared nothing; except being brought down behind the enemy lines.

Looking back on that slapdash, careless, nonchalant time, we seem to have been coldly efficient. We did our job to the best of our ability in what seem to be the craziest old antiquarian contraptions imaginable – the machines of the Royal Flying Corps. And we were up against an enemy that was ahead of us in aircraft design, and certainly not our inferiors in courage, elan and dash. And then suddenly it was all over.

The tumult and the shouting died, and there was I, with the remains of a war wound, a war gratuity and a war decoration, and with the wide world before me.

I also had two friends, ex-officers like myself, named Maddocks and Rendle – stout fellows both. We clubbed together and purchased two ex-wartime machines. DH6s, I think they were, and with these we carried on sundry commercial jobs, joyriding, taxi flights and so on.

We bought these machines very cheaply from Air Ministry war stocks, which were surplus to requirements, and as we crashed them we would dash back and buy others to replace the crashed machines. We were young and full of beans, and ready for anything. In fact, the new days of peace seemed strangely dull and flat after the old days of war.

One day I remember passing over some coverts, and with the 'war bird' fever still strongly working in us, we shot a brace of pheasants and landed to capture our bag.

The irate farmer suddenly appeared and accused us, not of shooting pheasants, but a hare, thereby breaking some ancient feudal law. The penalty for this, according to the farmer, was deportation or transportation for the term of our natural lives to

Australia, from which we had recently come to fight for King and country.

There was considerable excitement over the incident; the farmer declined to be mollified and we were 'taken to court,' as they say. Fortunately, another law intervened on our behalf. The prosecution could not prove that we had actually shot the hare, and the case was dismissed.

About this time we three became associated with the Blackburn Aviation Company.

The year 1919 had come in with a rush and, almost before we realised it, new marvels were being accomplished. Alcock and Brown had flown across the Atlantic; Harry Hawker had become a national hero, and to us, a tempting prize was held out by the Commonwealth government which offered £10 000 to the first Australian who should fly from England to Australia.

Ten thousand pounds seemed a lot of money to us. It *was* a lot of money. Furthermore, it was just such a venture as this that appealed to people like us and to others like us, too. There were dozens of Australian airmen in England at that time, and they all began feverishly to lay their plans for the flight.

Our idea was to fly in a Blackburn Kangaroo twin-engined machine, and it seemed a very good idea, too. But there was a nigger in the woodpile in the form of Mr. W. M. Hughes, our war time prime minister, who was all powerful in those days. When he heard of our plan, he put his foot down. We were too young; we were too inexperienced; particularly, we had no navigation knowledge or experience for such a tremendous journey. He absolutely forbade it and that was the end of our plan.

We sold the machine after an official veto had been placed on our venture by the Air Ministry. There was nothing else to be done, but a short time later two other Smiths, Ross and Keith, flew their Vickers Vimy out to Australia in 28 days, winning the prize of £10 000 and knighthoods for this magnificent feat.

My mind was filled with aviation to the exclusion of everything else. The fact was, though I did not realise it then, that the time had come when decisions were being made for me.

'... hanging by my legs from undercarriages' Smithy in California.

The course of my future left solid ground and soared up into the sky. But to where it would lead me, I had not the slightest notion. Having spent what little money I had, the pressing necessity arose of finding a job – obviously a job connected with aviation.

Looking for something that an airman could do, I heard of the great rich opportunities offering to bold young fellows who were ready to perform at Hollywood.

Stunt flying for film purposes was then in its infancy when I joined up with the film people, under contract as a 'stunt pilot' and 'wing walker', hanging by my legs from undercarriages. I very soon realised that my flying life would be short indeed if I continued at that game very long.

The people who attended these exhibitions were too bloodthirsty for my taste. They wanted too much for their money. They were not satisfied with flying and wing walking and other pleasant manoeuvres. I could see what they wanted. They wished to see a body or two carried off the field, and I did not want to be the body.

I felt, like Lord Clive, that I was reserved for something better.

Besides, the owners of the circus were unable to pay my wages, so I left.

There was, however, one further experience for me, before I left California to return to my native land. I undertook the role of 'Flying Scarecrow' on the rice patrol, a monotonous task of which I soon tired, of shooting duck from an aeroplane over the rice crops and spraying trees from the air. It was a sort of anticlimax to shooting down the Boche over the Western Front.

Leaving duck shooting to others, I took ship and returned to Australia – still seeking the elusive job.

By now I was an airman, a pilot whose destiny had already been decided. But aviation in Australia in 1921 offered little professional scope.

It would be untrue to say that there was no aviation in Australia in 1921; but there was very little of it.

A little group of Diggers, with more optimism than cash, had pooled their resources and started 'Diggers Aviation Ltd.,' a company formed to supply air services to the public, such as joyriding and taxi work. I worked with them for a time, and then I received an offer to join the newly formed West Australian Airways as a pilot.

West Australian Airways was a pioneering service, struggling along with inadequate capital. Nevertheless, it was an interesting time, including a forced landing on a very remote beach on the north-west coast. We were there for three days before being picked up, and we were so sunburnt that we were confined to bed in great pain for a week afterwards.

For two years I flew backwards and forwards on this service, covering thousands of miles, acquiring experience and gradually becoming bored with the monotony of it all.

Then I heard of a motor truck transport service operating from Geraldton and joined that as a working partner, but the West was no place in which to get on in those days.

'Go West, young man!' became for me 'Go East!' I had scraped enough money together to enable me, with my chum, Keith Anderson, to pick up a couple of old Bristol machines. We decided to fly these machines across Australia to Sydney, and off we went, taking each a passenger, one of whom, Mrs. Marshall of Cottesloe, was thus the first woman to fly across Australia.

Well, there we were in the big smoke of Sydney, stony broke, but with a fund of flying experience and a couple of old planes.

We had an idea of starting an air service to New Guinea, but there was not enough business offering in New Guinea then, though a few years later the discovery of rich gold put New Guinea on the map from an aviation point of view.

Meanwhile, the years were passing. This was 1927, and it was nearly ten years since the war had ended. I had nothing to show for those ten years which the locusts had eaten. It was time to be up and doing.

Knights of the Air

Mike Hayes

In World War I, when millions perished in the trenches, the loss of 9387 British and 8212 German flyers might not seem significant. But, bearing in mind the newness of aerial combat and the shockingly short lifespan of the majority of the combat flyers, the percentages are terrible. In some squadrons the casualty rates reached 98 per cent for an extended period. The rate for the entire war averaged 50 per cent. The life expectancy of a new pilot over the Western Front was three weeks.

The role of fighter pilots took some time to define. Originally the aircraft now generally regarded as fighters were scouts that did aerial reconnaissance. Then someone blazed away at someone else with a pistol or rifle. Someone else tried a machine-gun. The first recorded machine-gun killing was achieved on 5 October 1914 when French corporal Louis Quenault, observer in a French Voisin, shot a German Aviatik scout over Rheims.

Eventually a system was developed by which machine-guns could be synchronised to fire through the path of the aircraft's propellers without hitting and shattering the wooden blades.

Bombers graduated from dropping heavy debris and deadly little steel arrows, called *flechettes*, to dumping heavy bombs.

Australia's military aviation history began at Point Cook, on the shores of Port Phillip Bay, when the Central Flying School was established in 1914. By May 1915, four officers had been trained to fly, but Australia still didn't have any combat aircraft or enough manpower to make up a squadron.

The Australian Flying Corp's first foray into combat occurred when the Australian Half-Flight was posted to Mesopotamia in response to a call for help from the Indian Flying Corps to support them against the Turks in their attempt to capture Baghdad.

No aircraft could be made available by the British military, but four officers and forty-one aircrew went over and the Rajah of Gwalior bought two Caudron aircraft for them to use. Their early work was reconnaissance.

There were only four pilots, two of whom had just graduated from the fledgling academy at Point Cook in Victoria.

Australia's first air combat casualty occurred when one of the four flying officers, Lieutenant George Merz, a medical graduate

Office of Air Force History

'*Australia's first air combat casualty ... Lieutenant George Merz*'.

'In 1917, Lieutenant Frank McNamara became the first Australian airman to win a Victoria Cross'.

aged twenty-three, was returning to Basra after tending the wounded and sick in the hospital at Nasiriyah on 29 July 1915.

Merz had to put down in the desert due to engine failure and he and his New Zealand army passenger, Lieutenant Burn, were killed after a running battle with a band of hostile Arabs. They had only their revolvers as weapons but, according to eyewitness accounts, killed one and wounded five of the enemy in the gunfight.

By November 1915, only one of the original four Australian pilots sent to Mesopotamia with the 'half-flight' was left alive.

Later in the war, in 1917, Lieutenant Frank McNamara became the first Australian airman to win a Victoria Cross. Although severely wounded, he landed his Martynside single-seater in the desert next to the crippled BE2c of a comrade, Captain David Rutherford, to attempt a rescue. The citation reads:

> For most conspicuous bravery and devotion to duty during an aerial bomb attack upon a hostile construction train, when one of our pilots was forced to land behind the enemy's lines. Lieutenant McNamara, observing this pilot's predicament and the fact that hostile cavalry were approaching, descended to his rescue. He did this under heavy rifle fire and in spite of the fact that he himself had been severely wounded in the

thigh. He landed about 200 yards from the damaged machine,
the pilot of which climbed on to Lieutenant McNamara's
machine, and an attempt was made to rise. Owing, however,
to his disabled leg, Lieutenant McNamara was unable to keep
his machine straight, and it turned over. The two officers,
having extricated themselves, immediately set fire to the
machine and made their way across to the damaged machine,
which they succeeded in starting. Finally Lieutenant
McNamara, although weak from loss of blood, flew this
machine back to the aerodrome, a distance of seventy miles,
and thus completed his comrade's rescue.

Of course, most of the focus in World War I was on the Western
Front, and the Australian Flying Corps eventually sent three
squadrons there, to be absorbed into the British Royal Flying Corps.

There's a popular conception that the fighter skirmishes that
came to be called dogfights grew from a tradition somewhat akin
to gentlemanly duels in an earlier era. One suspects, however, that
this was just what today we would call 'hype'.

Harold Edwards was a member of Australian ground crew on the
Western Front and he had a very good reason to remember vividly
one of the war's flying legends, Baron Manfred von Richthofen.

'There's a popular conception that ...
dogfights grew from a tradition
somewhat akin to gentlemanly duels.'
Sopwith Camels and Fokkers.

'... one of the War's flying legends, Baron Manfred von Richthofen.'

Harold was a bit sceptical about the 'knights of the air' label attached by folklore to the dogfights. 'I think it was a very clever manoeuvre of the Germans', Harold said, 'to be able to get one or two of our airmen by themselves rather than meet a lot head on'.

It's interesting that one of our earliest combat aces, Captain A. H. Cobby, not only survived being attacked by five aircraft from Richthofen's Flying Circus in March 1918, but he and another pilot also managed to account for three of them. Cobby was our top ace. He shot down twenty-nine aircraft and thirteen balloons. He also went on to become one of the founders of the RAAF.

Harold Edwards' memories of Richthofen's last flight in April 1918 – now generally accepted (at least here in Australia) to have been the result of ground fire from Aussie trenches – show us that, despite the noble tag, death in the sky is just as pathetic and sad as it is anywhere else. Sportsmanship was a misplaced description of what went on.

> We used to see the Red Baron's three-decker plane, and there was a deal of 'scare' attached to him because he had the name of being a successful aeronaut. He certainly was a force to be reckoned with. But he had an umbrella, as I call it, of other aeroplanes all around him. He'd have eight to ten other planes making a great circus – we used to call it the Red Baron's Circus. Not infrequently he would be up very early in the morning. At daybreak you'd find this circus up in the air

*waiting for some of our people to come out, and then they'd
just sink down onto them and surround this one plane and let
the Baron have the pleasure of shooting him down.*

*We felt it wasn't fair sportsmanship. What it was, was war,
and as they say, 'all is fair in love and war'. We were more than
delighted when we heard Richthofen had been brought down.*

*As I understand it, he was following one of our aeroplanes
down. Our fellow dived to get away and he was following.
When they got down near the ground he levelled off. He had
flown some half a mile, or a mile, on the level, a few hundred
feet above the ground, when he was brought down. He
couldn't have done that if he'd been shot from above, but he
was shot by ground forces while he was on the parallel,
chasing our aeroplane.*

*Our squadron was commissioned to go out and collect his
crashed machine. When they got out to the scene of the crash
(it was in no-man's land and under pretty close observance by
the enemy) it was felt that it was not wise to attempt to bring
in the plane under the circumstances, so they decided to wait*

'… we used to call it the Red Baron's Circus.' Manfred von Richthofen in
the cockpit with his brother Lothar seated in front of the 'Flying Circus'.

until night. But in the meantime they wanted to get the body of Richthofen out, so one of our corporals, Corporal Collins if I remember rightly, went out with a rope and put it around the Baron's body so that by pulling the rope he could pull him out. Then they pulled the Baron's body to their cover and brought him back and Scotty Melville and I were deputed to take it in two-hour turns to guard the body in one of our hangars until the authorities had verified the authenticity of it being the Red Baron.

Richthofen was very poorly dressed. He didn't have any sort of coat on, just what I considered to be a rather shabby kind of shirt and an undershirt, a singlet. I was rather amazed that one in his position could be so poorly dressed.

He had a stern, set face it seemed to me and there were several marks, indentations and wounds. I could touch four or five on his face, but I didn't think any of them were bullet wounds. I felt they were wounds from the crash. What brought him down, undoubtedly, was a bullet that went through his right side, right underarm, and came out just in front of the left arm, just below the heart.

Harold's grisly assignment ended up in an incident which shows that the ultimate demise of the knights of the air could be anything but romantic. In fact, Harold's own personal standards and sense of morality were probably a bit more praiseworthy, and they had nothing to do with aerial combat.

After Scotty Melville and I had been looking after the body, we heard that the autopsy had revealed that Richthofen had been carrying 2000 francs in French money, in case he was brought down, to buy his way out. Scotty said he wished he'd known; he would have helped himself. When I told him what I thought of that, he wanted to fight me.

He said, 'If you feel that way about me, come back at four o'clock'.

I did, and blow me if he wasn't there standing waiting for me. I had to peel off and hop into him. That's the only fight I ever had.

When he saw a bit of blood from his own nose he didn't like it, because my arms were a bit longer than his.

The 'Red Baron' was buried by 3 Squadron Australian Flying Corps with the full military honours and a gun salute at Bertangles Cemetery, France on April 22 1981. Harold, being an instrument fitter, was deemed by the army to be just the man to engrave the nameplate for von Richthofen's coffin.

You do what you are told when you are in the Army or the Air Force. So I made up little engravers from bits of wire from the aeroplane's steel wires, polished them up and cut them suitably, then did the engraving.

Left: 'The Red Baron' was buried by 3 Squadron Australian Flying Corps ...'
Right: '... military honours and a gun salute.' Manfred von Richthofen's funeral.

No Time to Think: Three Aussie Air Aces of World War II

Mike Hayes

World War I established a popular stereotype for combat flying – and a lot of other rather unpleasant ways of killing or dying, as well. It also established an underlying terror, which plagued all combat pilots. It didn't matter which side you were on. At any one time, you just knew you were always going out to do battle with a foe that was undoubtedly better equipped than you. The only possible thing on your side was that maybe you were a bit more cunning or, hopefully, better trained.

Australian pilots seemed particularly impressed with how they'd been trained. Australia's highest scoring ace, Clive 'Killer' Caldwell, reckoned he first went into combat with only 150 hours flying time under his belt. Clive considered it totally inadequate. He honed his combat skills by flying 496 operational sorties in four theatres of war.

'Australia's highest scoring ace, Clive 'Killer' Caldwell.'

In the Middle East, where he first served, squadrons introduced raw pilots to combat situations by just 'chucking you in and seeing how you went'.

Had I gone to England, there were fighter Operational Training Units where they took you for six or eight weeks and showed you what they thought were the elementary basic ways of doing it. But we didn't have one in the Middle East. We just went and gave it a go, hoped for the best.

Bobby Gibbes was another World War II Australian pilot who felt he went into his first combat totally unprepared.

It was in Syria. In that show there were 1000 Ju-88s over the fleet off Haifa. We went in and attacked. The Navy put up a terrific amount of flak which we had to fly through to get at the Ju-88s. We managed to get to four 88s, which, incidentally, had Italian markings.

I suppose I felt apprehensive. I suppose I made a bit of a goat of myself really because I had never been to an OTU (Officer Training Unit) and I knew very little about combat flying. I didn't know much about the enemy aeroplanes that we were attacking. The Ju-88 was almost as fast as a Tomahawk. As I closed on the one I went after I wondered what all these little wispy things were – little smoke trails – going past me. I suddenly realised that they were bullets. I was being fired at. I thought, 'My God!'

Eventually I managed to stop that but I was covered with oil. I had attacked from behind. Pete Jeffrey, who was the CO, was a bit critical about that. Because I didn't know that the Ju-88 had a huge gun underneath, firing backwards as well. In fact I didn't know that I shouldn't have attacked from behind. I had never been told. The normal attack was the front quarter – head on, if you could – but never from behind.

Later I was shot down by a rear gunner on a Ju-88 flying over the desert. I was a fairly experienced pilot by then and CO of a squadron. The four Ju-88s were as fast as a Kittyhawk, which I was flying at that time. The only way

*I could get at them was to go in from behind. I think the one
I was shooting at ultimately went down. But in the meantime,
the guy on the starboard side set me on fire, so I parachuted.*

Clive Caldwell swore he went into that combat situation more
interested in seeing how he'd go than anything else. He couldn't
recall his first operational mission, but he certainly remembered
the first time he shot another aircraft down.

*I felt a bit sorry for him. I think he'd tried hard, hadn't seen
me in time. By the time he did see me, he was pretty heavily
damaged. On an occasion like that you keep on at him. He
only had one, or maximum two, other people with him, and
they were also fully occupied. So there was nothing very
spectacular about it, but I was glad to have done it, I don't
know why. Being frightened just didn't come into it.*

*Flying a fighter like that you haven't really got time to worry
about being frightened. What you worry about is
manoeuvreing the aircraft. You haven't got time to be
frightened and what's more, you don't hear anything except
the engine. If somebody is shooting at you, you don't hear it.
If they don't hit you, you don't know it's happened.*

Caldwell's particular talent seemed to lie in the fact that he was
an excellent shot. He was recognised as perhaps the best shot in
the RAAF. He admitted to being a fair enough shot before he
entered the air force. But the secret to combat accuracy was
something he called 'shooting at the shadows'. It's a theory that
came to mind in the Middle East when he sighted an unfortunate
dispatch rider.

*The poor fellow was riding a motorbike, doing his best, and
I thought, 'Well, by Christ! I'll shoot this fellow'.*

*All I had to do then to get him specifically was to put a little
more rudder on and hold it on him, and he had to get hit. If*

*you can hit what casts a shadow, that's the key. And so a good
clear shadow racing over the desert, or the smooth water of the
Mediterranean, registered very clearly. At a range of, say,
300 or 350 yards you put the whole of your burst into it in a
four-foot circle – there's the whole of your burst in to that.
And you need to be sure that you look before you fire, make
sure that you are clear, that your tail is clear, and that there's
not someone lining you up.*

*The big thing of the shadow firing was that you did things in
proper rotation: You can see the shadow. Then you've got to be
sure that you are really free to fire at it so that you can line it up
and concentrate on the range and your air speed and all the other
things that matter. Then open fire. Once you've fired your guns,
say, three seconds of fire, you must break away as though you
are now under attack yourself. Be sure you are clear before you
go back for more. The same with an enemy aircraft.*

Caldwell's technique didn't work for everyone. He recalled one
pilot who'd told him he used the technique and flew straight into
the sea because he was far too close to his intended target.
Nevertheless, in typical style, he pursued the matter with his
superiors, trying to get the 'kill' officially sanctioned.

When he took his squadron commander up to give him a go at
the new technique, his superior couldn't make it work. Caldwell
told him, 'On the evidence today, you couldn't hit a cow in the
arse with a bloody shovel'. Nevertheless, he passed on Caldwell's
ideas to Air Vice-Marshal Tedder who in turn issued an edict to
all desert squadrons to adopt the system.

Caldwell's main rival for the title of top Aussie ace was Bobby
Gibbes. He remained doubtful that the shadow shooting
technique was Caldwell's brainchild alone. But in his own self-
deprecating way, he didn't have big quids on himself either.

*Clive probably improved his marksmanship because of it.
I certainly didn't improve mine. I probably shot at more*

aeroplanes than Clive ever saw over there but I didn't get many. I was a poor shot. But air to ground, I think I was a very good shot. I could group my bullets to make them sure they didn't run through. I could hold them on the target while they went in to strafe but I certainly missed an awful lot of aeroplanes I fired at.

I think the classic was one day when I had a 'Kitty' Mark 111. I had a little bit more horsepower than the rest of the squadron. Three Messerschmitt 109s passed overhead, ahead of us. If I'd waited to take the squadron with me, which I normally would have done, they could have got away. Knowing I had a bit more power, I 'opened the taps' and went after them. I had a look at the three of them and thought, 'If I pull a lead one, the Number One, Number Three could probably get a deflection shot at me'. So I thought, 'I'll get Number Two first'. So I fired at Number Two. I must have misjudged their speed completely because the one behind – probably 50 yards behind – flicked over and went down smoking like hell.

I looked round to see who else had shot it, but I was the only one in the sky. I then decided I'd go after Number One and Number Two, but of course they didn't wait for me.

By the way, that Number Three did go down.

But there was something other than accuracy that separated a top combat pilot from the others. It wasn't just flying ability either. Other assessments of Caldwell indicated he was considered only an average flyer.

Clive hinted at another attribute which could best be described as knowing what your opponents did before they did it – a bit like replaying a video.

You get fairly used to what might take place, and if you've got a bit of an idea, then it does take place and you think, 'Well, I've seen this all before, I'll get this fellow'.

And if he's not particularly attentive to what he's doing, he gives you the opportunity. And if you shoot him, well, that's the end.

I might have been kidding myself but I did often feel 'This is a replay of what we've done before'.

Bobby Gibbes, who flew the same Middle Eastern theatre as Caldwell, didn't think he developed much of a sixth sense about what his opponents might do. He thought it was more about learning exactly how they thought tactically. Not that it always worked.

I think I knew exactly what my opposition (mainly the Germans, whom I was frightened of) were going to do. The Italians didn't worry us much. I came to a decision that no German pilot could shoot me down in a Messerschmitt. I knew their tactics completely.

The last time I was shot down was by a Messerschmitt 109!

It wasn't a lapse of concentration. I went down to rescue one of my people. I think I got the lead 109 that was beating him up, but his aircraft went in.

When I was catching up with the formation again, two 109s were picking at me. I was avoiding their attacks, evading them, climbing up to the formation, when somebody up above suddenly screamed out, 'Down below – look out!' I had lost sight of one of those 109s and I panicked. I pulled a full 360 degree circle, and of course I ran right into a 20 millimetre cannon shell and went down.

I always thought that the guy who screamed out to me to look out down below was the one responsible for shooting me down.

I managed to land, wheels up, at high speed with the two 109s right on my hammer. I thought they might beat me up but they didn't. Thinking they might strafe, I started to climb out as soon as I came to a stop, but they were gentlemen and flew past me, giving me either a salute or a wave.

The Middle Eastern combat also saw the Australians develop effective tactical flying, in terms of carefully executed formation flying. Bobby Gibbes describes one such formation devised by his squadron.

> We evolved a method of weaving for the whole squadron. We flew in pairs, weaving backwards and forwards behind each other, so we could pretty well cover the whole sky ahead, above, below or behind. And each one was keeping a pretty good look out. The Germans, by the way, called us the 'Waltzing Matildas'.
>
> It was a very effective formation. If an attack came in from behind, the lead who saw it would scream out, 'Duck!' We'd all do a 180 degree turn and when the German or Italian attack would come in, we'd all be facing them.

Also in the Middle East, Caldwell too was fighting both Italians and Germans. He found it also helped a little to know something about the character of your opponents.

> Oh, well, I'm sure the Italians were brave enough. They were keen on aerobatics. They would be above you, doing some very spectacular aerobatics. What that was supposed to do perhaps was impress you as to how dangerous they were. But one wouldn't question their courage.
>
> Well, I think the Germans thought they had a pretty good aircraft – and they did. I think they pumped the pilots up a bit and said, 'You're a hotshot, pal. Go and get them!'

In the Middle East, Caldwell commanded a Polish squadron, an experience which not only kindled in him an enormous respect for Polish fighter pilots but was also instrumental in him being awarded the Polish Cross for Valour.

> I had a high regard for them and thought they were a little bit over-brave maybe, or perhaps too optimistic. But you couldn't

complain about the Poles. They wanted to kill Germans.
They wanted to spend their day doing it.

About the only problem Caldwell had with his Polish crew was
that they often pretended they couldn't speak English, until he
mentioned over the radio that he'd just spotted an enemy aircraft,
then they understood perfectly and moved in for the kill.

To cure them of this habit, Caldwell announced that he was
grounding all the Polish pilots until their English improved.

> One of the worst things you can do with the Poles is not to let
> them fly. They want to fly all the time. All of a sudden their
> English became amazingly fluent.

Dealing with the Poles also allowed Caldwell to develop his own
quirky brand of international diplomacy.

> I'd hardly had the Polish squadron assembled with me, up in
> the desert area, and I got a signal from the Western Desert
> Headquarters to say,
>
> 'We're posting five Russian observers to you, and you'll
> give them accommodation and take them flying with you'.
>
> I couldn't get on the phone fast enough.
>
> 'What's wrong with you now?'
>
> I said, 'Gees, you are not sending me five Russians. They'll
> be murdered this evening'.
>
> 'Why should that be?'
>
> 'You know what the Poles think of Russians. I haven't got
> time to educate you in this sort of stuff. Don't send them out
> anywhere near here. Where are they?'
>
> 'On the road.'
>
> 'For Christ's sake, get somebody on a fast motorbike and
> turn them back. I won't be able to protect them. The Poles
> will just kill them. Surely if you find out what happened to
> Poland, and particularly the part the Russians played in it ...

you might know better. They hate the Russians just as much as they hate Germans. They'll kill them and there's no way I can stop them without them killing me too for sympathising with the bloody Russians.'

So anyhow, I sent a fellow down the road and stopped to catch the two trucks coming up and turned them back.

Caldwell wryly recorded how his Polish medal was personally presented to him at the Polish Embassy in London, while his Australian medals – the DFCs and DSO – were sent in the mail.

The concept of being thrown into the deep end to 'see how you went' continued when Caldwell was posted from the Middle East to England.

I was going to England from the Middle East, Tedder said to report to his headquarters, which I did. He said, 'You are going to England for experience'.

I said, 'Oh, I should get some there'.

He said, 'Well, it's in relation to Number 1 Fighter Wing, the Churchill Wing. And you'll be going back to Australia as wing leader'.

I said, 'It's a bloody fine thing to send me to Australia, to be a bloody wing leader in goddamn Spitfires. I've never even seen a Spitfire'.

'Oh, well', he said, 'you'll get one in England'.

I said, 'Gees, do listen to me. If I go to England to fly Spits I want to be plenty aware of what is going on'.

'You'll find it busy enough at Kenley Wing, I think, 11 Group – maximum effort.'

I said, 'Well, that's wonderful, but being a wing leader, all those under your leadership expect you to be experienced in the aircraft that you are dealing with, and if I'm not sufficiently experienced it's very unfair to them and quite unfair to me, to expect me to adequately handle a lead of an elegant wing like a Spitfire wing'.

'Yes,' he said. 'Well, we'll look after that.' So that's how it turned out.

Later, with No. 1 Fighter Wing in Darwin, Caldwell found himself in the position of actually leading his wing with his commanding officer flying under his leadership.

No. 1 Fighter Wing was commanded – very well too – by Group Captain A. L. Walters AFC. I thought him a first-class officer and an excellent chap. He didn't attempt to lead the wing. That was my job, because he hadn't had any operational experience. But he commanded the wing, and very well, in my opinion. And he flew on every operation. It didn't matter what it was, Wally Walters was somewhere on the formation.

He said to me, 'I'll be your number two'.

I said, 'Like bloody hell you will. I want somebody pretty sensitive who knows what they are bloody doing, and wants to stay alive, as my number two'.

'Oh, well', he said, 'we'll overcome that'. We did too, and I was very pleased to have him. He ended up shooting a Jap down in flames over Darwin – the plane went into the water there and I had a very good view of him.

I said to my number two on that particular day, 'Who's flying the Spit?' He said, 'I think it's Wally the One'.

'Is it? For Christ's sake!'

So I called Wally up. We used to talk about air tactics and that sort of thing, and I'd told him, 'Wally, keep your mind on the magpie. He comes in from behind you. He doesn't get you that time; he goes up and comes over and back again. He's always flying fast. Don't slow down in a turn with a Zero. They'll kill you if you do'.

So when I called him up on this occasion, I said, 'Wally, remember the magpie?'

He said, 'Yeah, don't bloody well interfere with me. This is my victim, you stay out of this'. Anyhow, he shot it down in flames – very good.

By Jesus Christ, it was only a few days later he was posted, promoted. Regular Air Force officers of his rank didn't fly. So that was the end of him.

Caldwell remained adamant that the same thing wasn't going to happen to him – losing his combat position and relegated to doing more deskwork. But he didn't realise the plan the air force had for him.

Wally came back from the interview at Air Force Headquarters Darwin – this was about ten o'clock at night.

'Have a drink', I said.

'Oh, for Christ's sake, let me rest,' he said, 'I've had a busy day.'

'So have I.'

He said, 'I'm posted'.

'I thought you bloody well would be. I told you never to tell them there what you are doing. They don't know and they resent it. There are group captains thick on the ground at headquarters. They won't like you butting in and doing this sort of thing.'

'Oh, well', he said, 'that's what I really thought was my proper duty. Aren't you interested in who's going to command the wing since I'm being posted out?'

I said, 'I couldn't give a damn who's going to command the bloody wing. I lead it, that's the important thing.'

'Well', he said, 'you are going to command it too'.

'I bloody well won't have that. I'm bloody well not going to do secretary work like that. Running around, like a clerk's job.'

He said, 'You can't dodge it, you are going to be CO of the wing.'

'As group captain?'

'Oh, no', he said, 'Lower rate of pay – wing commander'.

I said, 'That would be true Australian Air Force. That's true to the line.'

Despite his cynicism and lack of respect for authority, Caldwell took up his new posting. Although he tried to shunt off as much administrative work as possible to other people, he found there were some things he still had to do on top of his combat duties.

And despite his own fearsome reputation as a fighter pilot, he still worried about the inexperience and lack of preparation faced by his younger and newer pilots.

> *I was very concerned about these chaps. A lot of them had no experience at all. They came fresh out from England and they hadn't seen an enemy aircraft. So we had a sort of training aspect – 'Let's talk about what happens, how might it happen, the way it will happen', I said.*
>
> *'The whole thing depends on your attention and concentration. For Christ's sake, concentrate on what you are doing. Don't dream away about what it's going to be like when you get back on the ground. You will be on the ground the wrong way up, so for Christ's sake, think about it now. Now is the time!'*
>
> *We all got along very well. They seemed to trust me and I did the best I could for them. Simple.*

Caldwell's stint in Darwin allowed him to rack up a tally of nine Japanese aircraft destroyed. Officially, his total tally for the whole war was given as twenty-eight and a half kills, until more recent information indicated it should have been a whole twenty-nine. The update came in a letter from a man who, Caldwell believed, was the German ambassador to Italy after the war. He claimed Caldwell had shot down and killed his brother on Christmas Eve 1942.

> *Well, I did shoot an enemy aircraft – pretty heavily shot up. I put him in my logbook and claimed him as damaged because that, in my opinion, was all he was. But apparently he flew*

*on before his aircraft failed and he put down. He died 18 days
later in Italy, in hospital, with a shattered spine.*

*[In the letter] he said, 'I wanted to write to you to tell you, it'll
probably sadden you …', which it did. Christ, with a shattered
bloody spine! He had to take 18 days to bloody well die.*

Former Prime Minister Sir John Gorton knew first hand what it
was like to go down. He was originally diverted to Singapore,
instead of joining the rest of his squadron in Burma.

*We were going out with some other Hurricanes crated in the
hold to join them but on the way we got diverted to Singapore
and so we landed at Singapore and formed 242 Squadron.
I think it was the one we formed. I wasn't thinking that that
was going to happen when I left England.*

*The arrival of the 51 Hurricanes must have given some
military confidence to the locals in thinking they had some
advantage, but it was very misplaced confidence, because we
didn't have any ground control.*

*When an attack was developing from the air anywhere
around England we'd know it was coming. We'd be rung up
and told and we'd be able to take off and wait for them. Or
the squadrons could take off and wait for them in the air and
then attack them. But in Singapore we didn't have any ground
control like that. Most of the times the aircraft were overhead
before we even took off. That's no way to try and attack or
try and prevent an attack.*

The information they'd been given about their foe and the enemy
aircraft was hopelessly inadequate.

*Oh, there was a lot of nonsense about it. We were told they
had a thing called a Zero and they couldn't fly and the
Japanese had such bad eyesight that they could never be pilots.
That was just the way they felt about it, because they didn't
really know.*

RAAF Museum Point Cook

'Flying Officer John Grey Gorton.'

Within three weeks all but eight of the Hurricanes were destroyed. On 21 January 1942 Flying Officer John Grey Gorton became one of the statistics.

> *I can recall it quite well. Yes, my aircraft came down. It probably had bullets in it or something like that, but at any rate it wouldn't work. So I saw this place where I could come down and land and when I got very, very, very close to the ground I saw that it had some walls built between the tanks, petrol tanks which were stationed up and across. It was a tank farm [on Bintan Island, about 50 kilometres south-east of Singapore].*
>
> *I saw these walls but I couldn't do anything about it. I should have pulled the wheels up but I didn't because I tried to land so we could save the aircraft and get it out. The wheels hit and it turned over and flopped. I got my face all smashed in and everything like that.*
>
> *I remember thinking I had to get out of the plane, and opening the canopy and putting a hand down and getting out*

*and standing up. A fellow from some island was there with a
lot of Indonesian troops. They were shooting at me and he
stopped them. Then I just fell over because I had lost so much
blood. They took me to a man there who had some sort of
plantation. He looked after me as well as he could.*

*The RAAF sent a team out to get me with the aircraft.
They just looked at me and didn't do any good. They just
pinched my watch, my pay book and everything else and
cleared out back to Singapore.*

Relief finally arrived, and the badly wounded Gorton was
rescued. He had a fractured nose, both cheekbones were
fractured and he was wounded in both arms. Characteristically,
he questioned any suggestion that he also suffered severe shock.
The worst injuries were sustained when his face crashed into
his gunsight, probably because he wasn't properly strapped into
his cockpit.

His rescue could be described as ill-timed, because he was
transferred to the hospital ship *Derrymore* – a sitting duck in
Singapore harbour at the time the Japanese air attack was on.

*By that time it was really terrible because we were in the water
on the Derrymore and they were bombing us from
everywhere. The next day we got out and then Singapore fell.
We got down to somewhere or other and then got sunk.*

At 9 pm on Friday 13 February – an inauspicious date to say the
least – the *Derrymore* was torpedoed.

*At the time I was lying outside the pilot house and the torpedo
hit. We sort of bounced up and down and then there was
another roaring rush and the captain came out of the bridge,
grabbed the steward who was looking after him and they
jumped into the only lifeboat on board, dropped it and cleared
out. So we were all on board without a lifeboat.*

We had time to cut the hatches off and to get some stuff and floating wood and anything else that would float. She took a couple of hours to sink, I suppose.

We were floating around in the water and a submarine came through us. We couldn't see it but we could hear it. It didn't open fire on us and it went away.

Gorton and the others were in the water for about twenty-two hours, with no real food or drinking water.

We lost a lot of people when the ship sank. It was quite desperate. We could see all around there were things like aircraft tyres that were still floating there, and they'd have somebody lying on them.

So we were floating around on a sort of a raft thing that you could sit on, but there were so many people on it that you were in water. We saw some islands a little way away and tried to get to them, and then by pure accident the Ballarat came along – it wasn't looking for us.

On recovery, John Gorton was stationed in Darwin, this time flying Kittyhawks. There was no combat flying, only escort missions, but in September 1942 disaster struck again. He performed a forced landing on a beach on Melville Island. His aircraft was only slightly bent, but Gorton was forced to resort to a bit of bush tucker to survive.

Well, turtles came out of the sea, and came up under the wing of the aeroplane and dug a nest so I was very pleased to find them and dig them out. I also shot a swordfish, which was a remarkable feat. It was only small, but that helped a bit. And then Dickie Cresswell came across in an aeroplane and saw me.

Jolly John just couldn't stay out of trouble in aeroplanes. He tipped an aircraft at Brisbane and, on his next overseas posting to Milne Bay in New Guinea, he suffered engine failure again.

> *The engine cut out. It landed at the end of the runway, its wheels got caught and it tipped over. There were some anti-aircraft gunners there and they came out and started belting axes on the top of the thing. I shouted at them to stop because it was full of petrol and I was scared it might burst. Soon after that I was posted back to Mildura.*

The plight of the downed pilot was appreciated by all his mates. If you were unlucky enough to suffer such a fate, you could recover your good fortune if you had someone like Bobby Gibbes around.

On 21 December 1942 he picked up Rex Bailey, one of his pilots, in one of the Middle East war's most memorable acts of heroism. Gibbes was leading another five Kittyhawks on a reconnaissance mission to an Italian aerodrome called Hun. The famous Long Range Desert Group wanted an assessment made before they raided the base.

'... you could recover your good fortune if you had someone like Bobby Gibbes around.'

Office of Air Force History

Gibbes noticed a number of aircraft on the strip, so he ordered his pilots to strafe. Not a shot was fired in return, so they did a second run, which was wildly successful, with several parked aircraft and transports exploding and catching fire. During the run, Gibbes's aircraft ran straight through an exploding ammunition carrier. He knew his plane was peppered by shrapnel and feared his tail end might also have been damaged.

Nevertheless, when Rex Bailey was shot down about a mile from the strip, after an ill-advised third strafing run, Gibbes ordered the rest of his pilots to watch his back and he went in to the rescue.

Although Bailey advised him over the radio not to attempt a rescue, Gibbes found what he thought would be a safe landing spot about 5 km (3 miles) from the burning Kittyhawk. He called Bailey back saying he'd taxi as far as he could towards him, so in the meantime could Rex head out on foot.

> I started taxiing towards Bailey. I got part way – I suppose within a mile of him, two or three miles from the perimeter of the drome. I couldn't get any further, so I stopped the motor.

Gibbes realised he'd left himself little room to take off again, so he hung a handkerchief on a thorn bush to mark the absolute limit of his take off point. He spent the next little bit of time jettisoning his half full belly fuel tank and rolling it away from the aircraft, and he threw his parachute away to make room for Bailey, who eventually turned up.

> He climbed in and I sat in on top of him. I was as nervous as hell in case the engine wouldn't start, but it did. I stood on my brakes and gave it much more than normal power. Then I released the brakes and went staggering off towards this handkerchief, 300 yards away.
> I put down a little bit of flap and as I went past the handkerchief I still wasn't flying. We were thrown into the air. There was a ridge a couple of hundred yards further on. I hit

it with a hell of a bang. As I was thrown back into the air,
I saw my port tyre bowling along in the dust behind me.

The next ridge loomed up. It looked like I wasn't going to
clear it. I automatically put my right wing down, thinking that
maybe I could bounce it off on the one wheel. It didn't touch
and I got my under-cart up and kept going back towards base.

With Bailey having difficulty breathing because Gibbes was sitting
on him, they limped back to their headquarters at a place called
Marble Arch, about 300 km (190 miles) away. Luckily no enemy
planes approached them. After radioing to have emergency crews
standing by, Gibbes managed a one wheel landing. 'It was a
complete fluke on my part. I got away with it, but I shouldn't have.
I don't think I've ever been so frightened in my life.'

Typically, Gibbes was more impressed with the fact that his
aircraft was ready for combat again within a week than he was
with his own heroism. Not that his satisfaction lasted long. On a
mission flying escort for bombers, his squadron ran into some
heavy German fighter resistance and Gibbes was forced down
again. This time, although he escaped, the Germans burned his
much-cherished Kittyhawk.

Being shot at by all and sundry, having to kill to survive, facing
the continual danger of just falling out of the sky if your
equipment failed – they were all factors which, understandably,
led to a general dissatisfaction among Australian fighter pilots. It
is no surprise to learn that during the Pacific campaign some of
them actually went on strike. It's even less of a surprise to learn
that the irreverent 'Killer' Caldwell was one of the ringleaders.

Internal rumblings within the RAAF's top brass formed the
background to the dissatisfaction. There is also a suggestion that
the Supreme Commander of Forces in the Pacific, US General
Douglas MacArthur, engineered such instability to ensure his
greater control over the Australian air force.

From the combat pilot's point of view, it was really a matter of
not being happy laying down their lives for targets they didn't

consider worthwhile. Air Vice-Marshal Sir Valston Hancock gave this account of the pilots' dissatisfaction.

> *The pilots went on strike in effect. They rebelled. Strictly speaking they should have been shot for something like that in time of war. How they got away with it I don't know. Led mainly by Caldwell and a chap called Wing Commander Arthur, they felt that the targets allotted to them were not worth the metal and they were endangering their lives for no good pay-off. So they declined to perform.*
>
> *It was the subject of something pretty tantamount to a Royal Commission and the consequence was that Cobby was relieved of his command and went back to his job in civil aviation. Sims also, I think, resigned, and another senior administrative officer elected to take a reduction in rank to wing commander.*
>
> *I think Cobby and Sims spent too much time in their huts and not enough time talking to the pilots. Cobby had always been a lazy bloke. I was his adjutant for a couple of years and he'd be only too glad to let someone else do the work. But he was a very good leader. He had the capacity for talking people into doing things for him. He was a World War I Australian Ace, as a matter of fact.*
>
> *I believe there was justification, but you can't do it in war. Theoretically, there was every justification but, as I said, the* Manual of Air Force Law *provides that you are going to be shot if you rebel in times of war.*

Caldwell's attitude was that he believed a proposed landing at Tarakan was going to be a bloodbath, especially for his pilots, and he didn't want any part of it.

> *I was quite convinced that what we were about to put into practice would be a disaster. It was a fairly steep pebbly beach. You had to get in there and get off again. No sooner were you*

*on the beach, you had 30 or 40 foot of sandy rises. The enemy
were going to be on top of these and they'd slaughter you.*

*So I had a fair bit to say about it. I said, 'I will not take
command. You are not going to load this bloody thing onto me
at this stage of my life and have me condemned and damned
for a bloody failure. I don't mind operating, of course, but I
will not be the leader on the Borneo series. Tarakan can go to
hell, and so can you'.*

*We didn't have Tarakan until later on – and by gees, it was
a disaster. We were told we mustn't beat hell out of the bloody
landing ground at Tarakan because it was to be used by us.
But what bloody price do you pay to use a landing ground?
We could have gone and taken another one, or we were able
to fly direct from Morotai. Why pay such a high price? Here
fellows have been fighting all around the world for five years,
and they were going to murder them at Tarakan for nothing.
That's the view I took.*

It is interesting to read and hear other officers' opinions of
Caldwell, especially some of his superiors. While there's a distinct
respect for his combat record, it is often given grudgingly. His
disrespect for his superiors was returned in kind. Valston (Val)
Hancock regarded him as something of a con man.

*There isn't any doubt about his capacity for conniving, for
getting his own way. I'm just surprised he hasn't turned out to
be one of our high flyers today.*

Caldwell probably wouldn't deny charges of being able to wangle
special deals for himself. He was quite open about the time he was
court martialled for running his own sly grog business.

*Well, I think they were quite justified in doing so because
I was operating on a bigger scale than they were accustomed
to. I had my own personal transport aircraft, and I found that*

my superior officers – air commodores, air vice-marshals, and so on – were sending their aircraft down, ostensibly full of people going on leave, and going back up full of bloody grog. So I thought, 'If they can do it, why don't they do it on a proper scale?'

So I set mine off on a proper scale. I'd corner the market and control the price.

It wasn't well received.

The plan involved sending his Dakota transports back to Australia, loading them up with grog and selling them on a commercial basis to the Americans stationed around Morotai. The profits were good – it was possible to get £35 for a bottle of Australian whisky, tax free! And where did the proceeds go?

My personal account. I commanded, so it was for me. Purely and simply, it was for my own advantage. When my aeroplanes came in, by all means, come down and take a few cases out of that, mark it down for my credit if you please.

At the court martial on Morotai, Caldwell was totally unrepentant.

I said I thought we had many more important things to get on with, and if they couldn't bloody well discipline me and anybody else involved, the shortcoming was notable and it was their fault. In other words, I'll do what I bloody well like if it hurts nobody and is to my profit. I'm not in this bloody war for five and a half years for the fun of the thing.

'What do you mean?' they said. 'You don't command here.'

'Yes, I bloody well do. I command the fighter forces on Morotai, and I'll tell you this . . . I'll allow no aircraft in here without my approval. Understand that? We'll shoot them down.'

According to Caldwell, the court martial cost him a loss of rank, but he was remarkably vague as to actually what the penalty involved. He made light of the whole ranking system and claimed he didn't really know what rank he'd been or what it was reduced to.

What does it matter?

I might have been flight lieutenant, I'm not sure, I wasn't really very interested in the thing.

As a matter of fact, I thought I was an air commodore, and if you got access to the RAAF records you will find that in 1945 I was promoted to air commodore when I got back from the Philippines, and the air officer in charge there then said, 'You know, Caldwell, they've promoted you. Odd people, aren't they?'

I said, 'Promoted me? What to?'

'You are an air commode, a flying piss-pot now.'

I said, 'Is that right? Very appropriate too. While we're on the subject, pass the word back, "Not interested".'

'You are not interested?'

'I don't want any part of a continuing bloody love affair or otherwise with the RAAF, so forget it. I won't stay here a day longer than I have to, so I don't care whether I'm air commode or aircraftsman second class, I'm out, first opportunity. So pass the word back, it means nothing to me to be an air commode.'

'Well, it's a funny thing you know,' he said, 'most people would be pleased. You are the only bloody Empire Air Trainee that's become a bloody group captain, now you can be an air commodore and you don't want to be'.

I said, 'No, I've had enough of the whole thing'. So we let it lie at that.

And Caldwell's attitude stayed like that. Whether the attitude was contrived or not probably only matters in that it clearly illustrates the common stereotype of the combat pilot: the rebel, the cowboy, the larger than life character. When asked what he considered were the attributes of a first class combat pilot, Caldwell replied:

> I think what he required was to be lucky, and perceptive, and perhaps be given the opportunities. If, despite all that, he couldn't do it, he was out of his trade.
>
> I found a very surprising variation on the theme. Fellows I wouldn't have thought would have been able to beat bloody Mickey Mouse – they were bloody good fighter pilots. They had good perceptions, understanding of what they were doing. They were very alert, and they did well.
>
> I don't think there's any way you could tell what they were like till they got there and went through the crusher. That's the whole test. How do they behave under pressure? I was surprised how many did so well.

Bobby Gibbes always remained a bit more circumspect than Caldwell. He knew all too well how close he came to the emotional and psychological edge. Decades after the war he still showed a certain sad respect for fellow pilots drummed out of their units because they showed what was pompously and coldly referred to as 'LMF', lack of moral fibre.

The self-admitted nervous pilot who became a top combat performer and who led 3 Squadron – Australia's most decorated – knew all about the stresses of the job, and the qualities required.

> Reactions, for a start, have to be very fast. Invariably in combat you make instant decisions. I've been in pretty hectic combat and I've thought about it later, wondered if I did the right thing and I decided that I'd always been absolutely right in decisions I made on the spur of the moment.
>
> I think you have to be frightened. If you're not frightened, you're going to get yourself knocked down by being over-confident.

I think courage and cowardice are pretty much one thing in many ways. A pilot shows courage by doing things rather than be seen by his fellow pilots for what he really is – probably half a coward underneath. I certainly came into that category.

I went through two or three periods when I thought I just couldn't keep going. One day we had a combat and lost three of our pilots in the morning. In the afternoon I foolishly volunteered again to go out. I wasn't supposed to. I became the extra man – the 13th man – and when someone turned back I took his place.

We went through combat that day which lasted one hour and five minutes against the Germans.

We were over their territory and near their aerodrome. They could go back and refuel and rearm and come back. We had got into some extraordinary defensive circle and we basically weren't able to go anywhere.

We eventually landed back at a forward aerodrome coming on towards dusk, with the tanks almost empty and mainly out of ammunition. Next day I felt that I couldn't go on. I couldn't face it again. But I managed to hide that and I went out to the next show, which turned out to be a piece of cake. Then my morale improved again.

I went through two or three of these stages. I got to the stage once where I couldn't go to sleep. I was deliberately trying to stay awake so that I wouldn't have nightmares. That was a horrible stage. But I got over that and kept going.

I had nightmares in those combat situations – very much so. I still do sometimes. I have dreams of being behind enemy lines. I still get them, just occasionally.

Place an Arum Lily on My Grave

Jim Haynes

Pilot Officer Michael Dicken was on a training flight when he died. The accident that took his life occurred 15 miles out from Mildura airport, which was a pilot training centre during World War II. The crash took place near Iraak in far north-western Victoria.

Pilot Officer Dicken was just twenty years of age.

The Wirraway aircraft in which he was flying was seen to pull out of a steep dive and one wing broke off, causing the plane to crash into the ground immediately. Pilot Officer Dicken and his instructor, Flying Officer Power, were both killed instantly.

Michael Dicken's' short life was fascinating. His father was in the British Foreign Service and Michael was born in Egypt and raised in Morocco. It was there that he developed a love of arum lilies, which grew in profusion around his childhood home.

When war came in 1939 it was thought safest to send young Michael to far off Australia to complete his education. North Africa

Above left: ' … one wing broke off, causing the plane to crash into the ground.' The wreckage of the Wirraway in which Michael Dickin died.

Above right: 'Michael Dicken had a fascinating short life.'

was certainly not a safe place for a teenager during the war, nor was Britain during the blitz, so young Michael Dicken was sent to Melbourne Grammar School.

His father was posted to India soon after Michael left, so, when he finished school during the darkest hours of the war, there was no real option for Michael of making his way to his parents' new home. Instead he enlisted in the Royal Australian Air Force and was sent to Deniliquin where he completed the first stage of his service flying training.

It was at Deniliquin that Michael met a local girl, Joan Gooch. Michael and Joan became sweethearts and he told her many stories of his childhood in the exotic lands of North Africa. One evening he told her that, if he died during the war, he would like her to place an arum lily on his grave in his memory.

While Michael Dicken's background was exceptional, his fate, sadly, was all too common.

At No. 2 Operational Training Unit at Mildura alone, a total of fifty-two young men were killed in 45 accidents while engaged in pilot training during the desperate years of World War II. (The initial training in Wirraways carried two pilots – Kittyhawks and Spitfires one).

Those fifty-two young men were either training officers, repatriated from the war zones, youngsters who never had the

No 2 Operational Training Unit Museum, Mildura

'... *the well-kept graveyard where the crash victims were laid to rest*' .

chance to fly in combat and some straight from Service Training School, their young lives ending abruptly before they had an opportunity to fight.

That sort of thing happened all over Australia, of course. The difference is that Mildura has made a genuine, long-term attempt to remember the sacrifice of so many young lives.

As well as the well-kept Mildura War Cemetery where the crash victims were laid to rest, and the memorial in the Museum at Mildura, there are now granite memorials – with bronze plaques attached – at the various crash sites, each dedicated separately with a memorial service attended by the mayor of Mildura, local RSL Club chaplain, local historian Ken Wright, and any friends or relatives that can be traced.

The landowners on whose properties the crashes occurred were sometimes eyewitnesses and are also often present to pay their respects. Indeed, in some cases the land owners erected markers and memorials themselves and have kept the crash sites in good order to commemorate the victims.

During the war the owner of Keera Station, 30 miles west of Mildura, was Tom Grace. When two Boomerang training aircraft collided over his property and crashed, he erected crosses and planted two tamarisk trees in memory of the airmen who died.

Tom Grace and the owner of nearby Lybra Station, where the second plane crashed after the collision, joined the families of the two dead airmen, Flying Officers Syd Knapman and Roger Byrne, to place plaques at the sites. Subsequent owners of the properties continued to look after the sites. When the official memorials were unveiled over sixty years later, friends and descendants of the property owners, along with friends and family of the two airmen, including Flying Officer Knapman's widow, attended the memorial service.

The official memorials are the brainchild of Ken Wright OAM, who is one of a very few RAAF World War II flying veterans to still hold a pilot's licence. Ken is a past Mayor of Mildura and was also supportive of having the Museum set up at Mildura, in the reconstructed headquarters of No. Two Operational Training Unit.

It is no surprise to discover that many of the memorials are located beside Mildura airport or close by. Interestingly the very first memorial erected is actually within the city boundaries and marks the spot where Pilot Officer Macgowan crashed and died in a Kittyhawk. Three other fatalities occurred in the vineyard part of the municipality in January 1943 when two Wirraways collided over San Mateo and Etiwanda Avenues. Memorials now mark these sites. The instructor in one Wirraway, Flight Lieutenant Menzies, managed to use his parachute and escape.

'The Wirraway aircraft'. Michael Dicken died in a Wirraway.

It is, perhaps, typical of the people of a rural area like Mildura to want to remember the past in this fashion. Civic pride has always been strong in the city, which values its unusual history as an independent, planned and regulated town. The Canadian Chaffey brothers founded and planned the Mildura irrigation colony in 1887. Mildura became an oasis in the desert, Australia's first irrigated colony.

Civic minded individuals like Ken Wright are determined to see to it that the fifty-two young flyers who died in training at Mildura are not forgotten. The sadness that their deaths engendered among their friends and families, and also among the people whose lives they touched while training in Mildura and on whose properties they crashed, will be recalled when passers-by stop to read the plaques.

On occasions such as Anzac Day and Remembrance Day the plaques will serve as shrines and memorials to those men and many others like them who may not have died in battle, but who nonetheless gave their lives as a result of the call to duty and as a sacrifice to their country.

On 17 August 2004, on the roadside at Iraak, at a spot nearest to the crash site that is convenient for public access, Archdeacon Colin Tett dedicated a memorial to Flying Officer Power and Pilot

No 2 Operational Training Unit Museum, Mildura

'*After the ceremony, Mrs Ward planted an arum lily beside the memorial.*' *Mrs Joan Ward, Mildura Mayor, Peter Byrne and Ken Wright at the memorial dedication.*

Officer Michael Dicken. Among those in attendance were the mayor of Mildura, Peter Byrne, the instigator of the memorial scheme, Ken Wright, and Mrs Joan Ward of Canberra.

Mrs Ward's maiden name was Joan Gooch and, sixty-one years previously, while living in Deniliquin where she grew up, she had been the sweetheart of Michael Dickin. After the ceremony, Mrs Ward placed an arum lily beside the memorial and also another one on his grave at the Mildura War Cemetary.

PART 3

'ON TO AUSTRALIA' – FLIGHTS INTO HISTORY

Here are inspirational stories about the pioneers who flew through uncharted spaces to join Australia to the world … and survived to tell the tale.

It seems astonishing to the modern reader that Ross and Keith Smith needed 28 days to fly their Vickers Vimy from Britain to Australia in 1919. However, when you begin to consider the realities of the time: the type of machine they had for the task, the lack of runways and fuel along the way, the weather they had to endure and terrain they had to cross, you soon come around to being astonished at the immensity of their achievement.

Ross Smith and Charles Kingsford Smith belong to a bygone age; they are larger-than-life heroes of a type now rarely seen. Both were veterans of Gallipoli and both wrote fluent and erudite prose: original, fresh and poetic. Both also wrote in a style infused with a quiet nonchalance and understatement that belies the bravery and fortitude their actions displayed.

The cartoon which shows Bert Hinkler drawing Australia and Britain closer together is a telling reminder of how these flights were seen at the time they were made. These flyers were intrepid heroes to be likened to Da Gama, Magellan and Cook.

Australia's isolation from the rest of the world in general, and the English speaking world in particular, is something of which we are still aware today, but we can have little idea how much stronger that feeling was before these flights were made and aviation developed into the phenomenon we know today.

Like Cook and Magellan before them, most of these heroes died in the course of their explorations. Smithy disappeared over the Bay of Bengal, Ulm disappeared over the Pacific, Ross Smith died in a crash while testing a new aircraft in Britain, Hinkler crashed to his death in a remote Italian mountain range, Amy Johnson died when the plane she was delivering went down into the Thames Estuary. Like the shooting stars they were often likened to, they shone brightly for all too brief a time.

A Magnificent Undertaking

Jim Haynes

PART I — THE RIGHT MAN

There was probably no better example of what a fighting
airman should be like than the Australian, Ross Smith.
Like many of the successful airmen of the Australian Flying
Corps, Ross Smith came from the Australian Light Horse.

(Official Australian War History)

Captain Ross MacPherson Smith (Knight Commander of the Order of the British Empire, Air Force Cross [twice], Military Cross [twice], Distinguished Flying Cross [three times]) was born in Adelaide, in 1892.

A gifted athlete and horseman, he enlisted as a trooper in the 3rd Australian Light Horse at the outbreak of war in 1914. All eleven members of the school cricket team, which Ross had

14,000 Miles Through the Air Ross Smith

'There was probably no better example of what a fighting airman should be like.' Sir Ross Smith in uniform.

captained, enlisted. Five were killed, including his younger brother Colin, and another five were wounded.

Ross's elder brother, Keith, was rejected by the AIF because he had varicose veins. Keith had the veins surgically removed, made his way to Britain and joined the Royal Flying Corps.

Ross Smith served at Gallipoli and was promoted to regimental sergeant major in August 1915 and commissioned as a second lieutenant in September, just as he was evacuated from Gallipoli with enteric fever.

He spent six months recovering, then was given command of a machine-gun section in Egypt in early 1916, fought at the decisive Battle of Romani, and decided to join the Australian Flying Corps.

He began training in Cairo in October 1916, receiving his observer's wings in January 1917 and pilot's wings in July 1917.

Despite starting so late and spending most of his time with No. 1 Squadron, which was a bomber and reconnaissance unit, he finished the war as Australia's tenth top pilot for confirmed 'kills' in air combat and was decorated for gallantry five times between January 1917 and November 1918.

> *The watcher on the tower yelled 'Aeroplane up!' One enemy two-seater and three scouts were coming . . . Ross Smith, with his observer, climbed like a cat up the sky . . . fastened on the big one, and, after five minutes of sharp machine-gun rattle, the German dived suddenly towards the railway line . . . Five minutes later Ross Smith was back. Our sausages were still hot; we ate them and drank tea. Ross Smith wished he might stay forever on this Arab front with an enemy every half hour.*

(T. E. Lawrence *The Seven Pillars of Wisdom*)

Ross flew Lawrence of Arabia on secret missions into the desert and gained expertise with all kinds of aircraft including Bristol fighters, various prototypes called 'British Experimentals' (christened 'Bloody Emergencies' because of their unreliability), and the lumbering HP100 heavy bomber, made by Handley-Page.

His experience with the HP100, which could carry a ton of bombs over long distances, was to change his life and turn him into a legend.

After the Armistice, Ross Smith made the first flight from Cairo to Calcutta in the HP100, with Brigadier General Borton and sergeants Wally Shiers and Jim Bennett. Intending to fly on to Australia, they travelled as far as Timor by ship to check for landing places and talk to the Dutch colonial authorities. Meanwhile the HP100 was flown to the north-west frontier to deal with an Afghan uprising and crashed in a storm.

They had abandoned the idea of flying to Australia when a chance acquaintance showed them the first Australian newspaper they had seen in five years. On the front page was an offer made by Prime Minister Billy Hughes of £10 000 to the first Australian air crew to fly a British aircraft from England to Australia in less than thirty days.

Part 2 — The Great Race

Hundreds of Australians attempted to enter the race. The Australian government recruited the Royal Aero Club as arbiters and organisers. The rules were strict in order to avoid the government being criticised for putting lives in danger.

The aircraft entered had to be airworthy. This meant in effect that only an aircraft entered by a manufacturer was acceptable. Most would be entrants could not afford new machines.

Each crew had to have a navigator, which eliminated the entry put up by Charles Kingsford Smith, and solo entries were forbidden by the regulations, so Lieutenant Bert Hinkler's entry in a Sopwith Dove was also eliminated.

National Archives of Australia

'The sixth crew, Lieutenants Ray Parer and John McIntosh.'

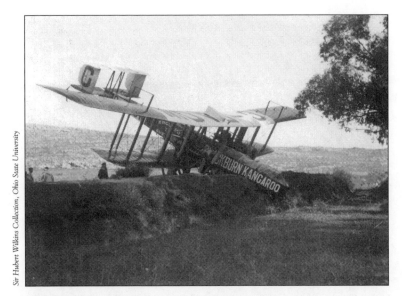

Sir Hubert Wilkins Collection, Ohio State University

'The Blackburn Kangaroo ... was forced to turn back to Crete ... and crashed on landing.'

Ross Smith knew somebody who really could navigate and who could also share the burden of flying the machine – his own brother, Keith, an RFC and RAF flying instructor who was still based in Britain and available to take part in the venture.

Altogether six Australian crews, five of them backed by the cream of the British aircraft industry – Sopwith, Vickers, Blackburn, Alliance and Martinsyde – took part in the race. The sixth crew, lieutenants Ray Parer and John McIntosh, after months of setbacks and failed schemes, were backed by Scots whisky magnate Peter Dawson and had entered a war surplus de Havilland DH-9, which they named 'PD' in his honour.

There was also an unofficial seventh entry. French flyer Etienne Poulet and his mechanic, Jean Benoist, flying a tiny Caudron G4 biplane, set off from Paris on 14 October 1919. Not being Australian, they were ineligible for the cash prize, but they were determined to win the race, and the glory, for France. They were to lead the race for over half the distance.

Of the seven entrants only two would reach Australia.

A Magnificent Undertaking ~ 117

'Parer and McIntosh ... arriving in Darwin eight months after leaving London.'

The Smiths' Vimy took off from Hounslow Heath at 9.05 am on 12 November 1919.

They flew up to ten hours each day, then Shiers and Bennett would work on the Rolls-Royce engines while Ross and Keith refuelled, straining petrol through a chamois leather filter. They followed this routine for twenty-seven days.

Of the other entrants, two crashed fatally: the Alliance Endeavour, flown by Douglas and Ross, just after taking off from Hounslow, and the Martinsyde, flown by fighter ace Cedric Howell and George Fraser, when it ditched off Corfu in the Adriatic Sea after a navigation error during the night.

The Blackburn Kangaroo of Captain Sir Hubert Wilkins was forced to turn back to Crete with engine trouble and crashed on landing, while George Matthews and Tom Kay in the Sopwith Wallaby made it all the way to Bali, where they crashed in a banana plantation.

Poulet and Benoist in their Caudron just kept plugging away and led the field as far as Rangoon before they too were eliminated with engine trouble.

The astonishingly determined Parer and McIntosh limped from one near disaster to another in their single-engined DH-9 eventually arriving in Darwin eight months after leaving London. Their flight was the first to Australia in a single-engined plane.

The biggest problem for the competitors was that there were no landing grounds between India and Darwin. There wasn't even a landing ground at Darwin until the race was underway.

The Dutch had set up a couple of flying schools in the Dutch East Indies (Indonesia) and constructed rudimentary airstrips during 1919, but elsewhere most 'airfields' consisted of racecourses like those at Rangoon and Singapore or clearings in the jungle with a stockpile of fuel.

The Vickers Vimy touched down on the specially built Fanny Bay airstrip near Darwin at 3.40 pm on 10 December. Her tanks were almost empty. 'We almost fell into Darwin', Wally Shiers recalled many years later. The journey had taken twenty-seven days and twenty hours.

14,000 Miles Through the Air Ross Smith

'The Vickers Vimy touched down ... near Darwin at 3.40 pm on December 10th.'

Waiting to greet them were a customs officer, a quarantine official and Ross Smith's old friend from the No. 1 Squadron Australian Flying Corps, Hudson Fysh, who had built the airfield at Darwin and surveyed the air route from Darwin to Brisbane, in case anyone got that far.

It was this survey that convinced Fysh that air travel was the answer to Australia's vast distances and led directly to the formation of Qantas.

Brigadier General Borton called the flight 'the most magnificent pioneer undertaking of the age' and British Prime Minister Lloyd George telegrammed: 'Your flight shows how the inventions of war can advance the progress of peace.'

God 'Elp All of Us

Ross Smith

PART ONE:
'LET'S FLY ON TO AUSTRALIA
AND SEE THE MELBOURNE CUP'

I made the first aerial voyage from London to Australia largely due to the experiences gained piloting a Handley-Page aeroplane towards the end of the war. At that time I was with the Australian Flying Corps as part of General Allenby's last offensive in Palestine, to take part in night bombings.

The remarkable success of this terrible engine of destruction, and its unfailing reliability during long-distance flights, opened my eyes to the possibilities of modern aeroplanes and their application to commercial uses.

The trip itself was first suggested in a joke.

Brigadier General Borton invited me to join him in a flight to link up the forces in Palestine with the army in Mesopotamia. After reaching Baghdad, we would find a route to India, 'to see,' he jocularly remarked, 'the Viceroy's Cup run in Calcutta.'

'Then, after that,' I replied sarcastically, 'let's fly on to Australia and see the Melbourne Cup!'

So it eventuated that on 29 November 1918, just after the Armistice was signed, Borton and RAF Commander Major-General Salmond, took off from Cairo in the Handley-Page, accompanied by myself and two air mechanics, Sergeants Bennett and Shiers.

It took just three weeks to pioneer a route to India, where we arrived, on 10 December 1918, scarcely a month after the signing of the Armistice (and in time to attend the Viceroy's Cup Race Meeting).

This was the longest flight that had been made up to this time, and it convinced me that a well-equipped and serviced plane was capable of flying anywhere, given suitable landing grounds.

In India, General Borton chartered a steamer, the RIMS *Sphinx*, intending to explore the route to Australia, arrange suitable landing grounds, return to India, and fly to Australia over the established course. I accompanied him.

We sailed from Calcutta on 10 February 1919, with stores and equipment and 7000 gallons of petrol. We intended to dump 200 gallons of petrol at each suitable landing place along the anticipated flight route.

Two days later, just after leaving Chittagong, our first port of call, the *Sphinx* caught fire and blew up. We lost everything but our lives.

We returned to Calcutta where the Indian government generously lent us another vessel, the RIMS *Minto*. This time we carried no petrol.

Our three month expedition visited Burma, the Federated Malay States, the Netherlands Indies, Borneo and Siam but on our return we found that the Handley-Page had been crashed in a storm in the North of India.

Then we learned that the Australian Commonwealth Government had offered a prize of £10 000 for the first machine, manned by Australians, to fly from London to Australia in 30 days.

General Borton, not being an Australian, was ineligible. He nevertheless approached the Vickers company to supply a machine for me to fly.

In England my brother Keith was awaiting repatriation to Australia. He had been flying with the Royal Air Force and had gained extensive and varied air experience. He signed up as assistant pilot and navigator. Sergeants Bennett and Shiers agreed to accompany us as air mechanics, making a crew of four.

There was limited preparation time. Winter was fast approaching. Long distance flying would soon be extremely unpleasant and four other competitors were ready to start before the Vickers machine was even handed over to us.

Shell agreed to have petrol supplies at the required depots and Wakefield Ltd undertook to arrange oils. From Darwin the Defence Department of Australia had made all necessary arrangements.

The challenge was to reach Australia.

The route I decided upon was, roughly, England, France, Italy, Crete, Egypt, Palestine, Mesopotamia, Persia, India, Burma, Siam, Federated Malay States, Dutch East Indies to Port Darwin.

The machine was a Standard Vickers Vimy bomber with an extra petrol tank.

It was powered by two 360 horsepower Rolls-Royce Eagle VIII engines. The wingspread was a little over 67 feet and the total weight, loaded, was six and a half tons. Our petrol capacity would carry us for 13 hours at a cruising speed of 80 miles an hour – ample for the longest stages between aerodromes.

Great enthusiasm was shown by the employees of Vickers in the fitting, testing, and final adjusting. They were providing more than labour, producing from their factory an ideal to uphold national prestige. Thus we were able to place the deepest confidence in the machine and hundreds of times during the flight we had occasion to pay tribute to and praise the sterling efforts of those British workers.

My brother took care of maps. Wherever possible, we would fly our course by maps and direct observations of features on the ground; but when cloudy or misty weather obscured terrestrial observation, we would rely solely on navigation. We had an

Admiralty compass, a ground-speed and drift indicator, and our own flying experience to fall back on.

We discussed at some length carrying a wireless set and finally decided not to take one. It would weigh 100 pounds, take up a good deal of room and be of little use except for sending cheery messages to various places we passed over.

I had been from England to Australia several times by mail steamer, embarking either at Tilbury or Marseilles and, in due course, reaching Adelaide with little thought about the journey.

This time we had an aeroplane at Brooklands aerodrome and somewhere away on the other side of the world was Australia. We were going to climb up into the air and *fly* through thousands of miles of space to our own home!

It was to be a great adventure – this skimming through 'unflown skies', over strange lands, and vast spaces of ocean. We were attempting something which had never before been done, so it is no wonder that we went about our work with eagerness and light hearts.

I knew that the physical and nervous strain of long flying hours day after day would be great so we all went into training and generally took care of ourselves. At night we would work on the maps, plotting out the course and studying the prominent landmarks. Long before we left England, we had visualized most of the country that we were to fly over.

For food we carried an emergency ration of tinned meat and biscuits, along with chocolate and Bovril. Roughly, we had enough food to last us seven days. We expected to get food to last us for the next day at each place at which we landed. We carried a fishing line and a few hooks in case we should land on some small uninhabited island and have to do the 'Robinson Crusoe' act for a time.

As we were to fly over several foreign countries, the International Air Convention required that we should have a distinctive number or mark painted on the machine, just as a motorcar has to carry a number plate.

14,000 Miles Through the Air Ross Smith

'The Air Ministry allotted us the letters 'G-E A O U,' which were painted on the wings and fuselage … 'God 'Elp All Of Us!' '

The Air Ministry allotted us the letters 'G-E A O U', which were painted on the wings and fuselage, the 'G' standing for Great Britain and 'E A O U' representing our number.

In view of the long flight our own interpretation of this marking was 'God 'Elp All of Us'!

Part Two:
Through the Cloud Ocean

To give our supplies of fuel and oil time to reach some of the more remote aerodromes we stayed a week in England after the Vimy was tested by Sir John Alcock and pronounced fit.

The weather during this week's stay was abominable. Winter was fast closing in with typical English November fogs. Driving sleet and pelting rains fell almost without intermission.

On the morning of November 12th we were called at 4.30 am and I was delighted to find a clear, frosty morning. However, at 6.30 am a dense ground haze appeared, and weather reports sent

National Archives of Australia

'... a crew of four.' Left to right: Wally Shiers, Keith Smith, Ross Smith,
Jim Bennett.

by the Air Ministry forecast bad weather in the southeast of
England and the north of France.

The machine was run out from the hangars and Commander
Perrin, of the Royal Aero Club, marked and sealed five parts of it,
in accordance with the rules of the competition. Three of the
marked parts had to be produced upon arrival in Australia, in
order to identify the machine.

At eight o'clock the forecast was 'totally unfit for flying' but our
minds were made up and, come fair, come foul, we were
determined to start. A few friends had gathered to bid us God
speed, and, with their kindly expressions and cheers sounding in
our ears, we climbed into our seats and took off from the snow
covered aerodrome.

We climbed slowly upward through the cheerless, mist laden
skies, our engines well throttled back and running perfectly. To
make sure, we circled for ten minutes above Hounslow, then set off.

At 2000 feet we emerged from the fog belt into brilliant
sunshine, but the world below was lost to sight, screened by the

14,000 Miles Through the Air Ross Smith

'*The machine was run out from the hangars ...*' *The Vimy ready to leave Hounslow.*

dense pall of mist. We set a compass course for Folkestone and just before reaching its outskirts a rift in the mists enabled us to pick up the grand old coastline.

The frigid breath of winter stung our faces and chilled us through; its garb of white had fallen across the land making the prospect inexpressibly drear. The roadways, etched in dark relief, stood out like pencil lines on the snow clad landscape.

It seemed hard to realize that we had at last started out on the long flight for which we had been planning and working so long, and as I glanced over the machine and the instruments I wondered if the fates would be so kind as to smile on us ever so little and allow us to reach the goal of our ambitions . . . Australia in thirty days.

The machine was flying stately and steady as a rock. All the bracing wires were tuned to a nicety; the daub on the huge planes glinted and glistened in the sunlight; I was filled with admiration. The engines, which were throttled down to about three-quarters of their possible speed, had settled down to their task and were purring away in perfect unison and harmony.

A small machine is ideal for short flights, joyriding the heavens or sightseeing among the clouds; but there is something more majestic and stable about the big bombers which a pilot begins to love.

A flying machine is something so entirely apart from and above all other contrivances of man's ingenuity. The aeroplane is the nearest thing to animate life that man has created. In the air a machine ceases indeed to be a mere piece of mechanism; it becomes animate and is capable not only of primary guidance and control, but actually of expressing a pilot's temperament.

The lungs of the machine, its engines, are almost as awesome as the human anatomy. When both engines are going well and synchronized to the same speed, the roar of the exhausts develops into one long-sustained rhythmical boom – boom – boom. It is a song of pleasant harmony to the pilot, a duet of contentment that sings of perfect firing in both engines and says that all is well.

This melody of power boomed pleasantly in my ears, and my mind sought to probe the inscrutable future, as we swept over the coast of England at 90 miles per hour.

And then the sun came out brightly and the Channel, all flecked with white tops, spread beneath us. Two torpedo boats, looking like toys, went northward. And now, midway, how narrow and constricted the Straits appeared, with the grey-white cliffs of old England growing misty behind, and ahead – Gris Nez – France, growing in detail each moment!

I was beginning to think that the official prophet, who had predicted bad conditions at our start, was fallible after all. It was not until we reached the coast of France that the oracle justified itself; for, stretching away as far as we could see, there lay a sea of cloud. Thinking it might be only a local belt, we plunged into the compacted margin only to discover a dense wall of nimbus, heavily surcharged with snow.

The machine speedily became deluged by sleet and snow. It clotted up our goggles and the windscreen and covered our faces with a mushy, semi-frozen mask. Advance was impossible and so we turned the machine about and came out into the bright sunshine again. We were then flying at 4,000 feet, and the clouds were so densely compacted as to appear like mighty snow cliffs, towering miles into the air.

There was no gap or pass anywhere, so I shut off the engines and glided down, hoping to fly under them. Below the clouds snow was falling heavily, blotting out all observation beyond a few yards. Once more we became frozen up, and, as our low elevation made flying extremely hazardous and availed us nothing, I determined to climb above the cloud mass and, once above it, set a compass course for Lyons.

Aerial navigation is similar to navigation at sea, excepting that the indispensable sextant is more difficult to use in the air, owing to the high speed of travel and the consequent rapid change from place to place and for other technical reasons. Allowances have also to be made for the drift of the machine when side winds are blowing – an extremely difficult factor to determine accurately.

The Air Ministry had furnished us with charts indicating the trend of the winds and their approximate force at various altitudes, so we knew, roughly, what allowances to make in our dead reckoning if we lost sight of the ground.

We climbed steadily in a wide, ascending spiral until we reached an altitude of 9000 feet, and were then just above the clouds. Below us the snowstorm raged, but we had entered another world – a strange world, all our own, with bright, dazzling sunshine.

The mighty cloud ocean over which we were scudding resembled a polar landscape covered with snow. The rounded cloud contours might have been the domes of snow-merged summits. It was hard to conceive the amorphous expanse was not actual, solid. Here and there flocculent towers and ramps heaved up, piled like mighty snow dumps, toppling and crushing into one another. Everything was so tremendous, so vast, that one's sense of proportion swayed uncontrolled.

There were tiny wisps, more delicate and frail than feathers while chasms thousands of feet deep, sheer columns and banks extended almost beyond eye reach.

Between us and the sun stretched isolated towers of cumulus, thrown up as if erupted from the chaos below. The sunlight, filtering through their shapeless bulk, was scattered into every conceivable gradation and shade in monotone. Round the margins the sun's rays played outlining all with edgings of silver.

The scene was one of utter bewilderment and extravagance. Below, the shadow of our machine pursued us, skipping from crest to crest, jumping gulfs and ridges like a bewitched phantom. Around the shadow circled a gorgeous halo, a complete flat rainbow. I have never seen anything in all my life so unreal as the solitudes of this upper world through which my companions and I were now fleeting.

My brother worked out our course, and I headed the machine on to the compass bearing for Lyons; so away we went, riding the silver edged sea and chased by our dancing shadow.

For three hours we had no glimpse of the earth, so we navigated solely by our compass, hoping eventually to run into clear weather, or at least a break in the cloud, so that we might check our position from the world below. My brother marked our assumed position on the chart, by dead reckoning, every fifteen minutes.

The cold grew more intense. Our hands and feet lost all feeling and our bodies became well nigh frozen. The icy wind penetrated our thick clothing and it was with greatest difficulty that I could work the machine. Our breaths condensed on our faces and face masks and iced up our goggles and our helmets.

Occasionally immense cloud barriers rose high above the lower cloud strata, and there was no circumventing them; these barriers were invariably charged with snow, and as I plunged the machine into them, the wings and fuselage were quickly armoured with ice. Our air speed indicator became choked and we ourselves were soon covered white by an accumulating layer of driving snow. Goggles were useless, owing to the ice, and we suffered much agony through being compelled to keep a lookout with unprotected eyes straining into the 90-miles-an-hour snow blast.

When I suggested to my brother that we should have some sandwiches for lunch, we discovered they were frozen hard.

Fortunately, we carried a thermos flask of hot coffee and the *piéce de résistance* was a few sticks of chocolate, part of our emergency rations. I have never felt so cold or miserable in my life as I did during those few hours.

My diary is terse, if not explicit:

> *'This sort of flying is a rotten game. The cold is hell and I am*
> *a silly ass for having ever embarked on the flight.'*

We were quite uncertain as to our location, and I had visions of what would happen if we encountered a heavy side wind and got blown into the wild Atlantic.

The only really cheerful objects of the whole outfit were our two engines. They roared away and sang a deep throated song, filled with contentment and gladness; it did not worry them that their radiator blinds, which we kept shut, were thickly coated with frozen snow. I regarded those engines with envy. They had nice hot water circulating around them, and well, indeed, they might be happy. It seemed anomalous, too, that those engines needed water flowing around their cylinders to keep them cool, while we were sitting just a few feet away semi-frozen. I was envious!

The situation was becoming desperate. My limbs were so dead with cold that the machine was almost getting beyond my control. We must check our position and find out where we were at any cost.

Ahead loomed up a beautiful dome shaped cloud, lined with silver edges. It was symbolical; and when all seemed dark, this rekindled in me the spark of hope. By the side of the 'cloud with the silver lining' there extended a gulf about two miles across. As we burst out over it I looked down into its abysmal depths.

As far as the eye could reach, in every direction stretched the illimitable cloud sea and the only break now lay beneath us.

It resembled a tremendous crater, with sides cleancut as a shaft. At the bottom lay the world.

Down this wonderful cloud avenue I headed the Vimy, slowly descending in a wide spiral. The escape through this marvellous gateway, seven thousand feet deep, that seemed to link the realms of the infinite with the lower world of mortals, was the most soul stirring episode of the whole voyage.

Snow was falling heavily from the clouds that encircled us, yet down, down we went in an almost snow free atmosphere. The omen was good; fair Fortune rode with us. The landscape was covered deep in snow, but we picked out a fairly large town, which my brother at once said was Roanne. This indicated that we were directly on our route; but it seemed too good to be true, for we had been flying at over 80 miles per hour for three hours by 'blind navigation' and had been unable to check our course.

At 1000 feet I circled above the town. Our maps informed us that it was Roanne! Lyons, our destination, was only 40 miles away.

Exquisitely indeed is the human mind constituted; for, now that we knew where we were, we all experienced that strange mental stimulus – the reaction, after mental anxiety and physical tribulation. We forgot the cold, the snow, the gloom; everything grew bright and warm with the flame of hope and success.

And so eventually we reached Lyons and landed.

I have always regarded the journey from Hounslow to Lyons as the worst stage of the flight, on account of the winter weather conditions. We had flown 510 miles on a day officially reported 'unfit for all flying'. Furthermore, we had convinced ourselves that, by careful navigation, we could fly anywhere in any sort of weather, and we had gained absolute confidence in our machine and engines.

We were so stiff with cold when we climbed out of the machine that we could hardly walk. But what did it matter? Our spirits ran high; we had covered the worst stage; the past would soon be forgotten, and new adventures lay awaiting us in the near, the rosy, future.

The French flying officers were very surprised when they learned we had come from London. They looked up at the weather, at the machine, then at us, and slowly shook their heads. It was an eloquent, silent expression. They were still more surprised when they learned that we intended leaving for Rome the next morning.

Not one of us could speak French very well, and we had considerable difficulty in arranging for petrol supplies to be delivered to the machine by next morning. Sergeants Bennett and Shiers just had time to look over the engines before the winter darkness settled down. We all turned into bed very early, very tired, but very happy.

On opening my personal kit that night I found it, too, had suffered the rigours of the sky journey. It was still frozen stiff – my solitary toothbrush!

PART THREE:
A PASS IN THE MOUNTAINS

It was a frosty daybreak, and for a short time after takeoff we encountered some clouds; but as we progressed these drifted away, clearing the atmosphere and unfolding a scene of bewildering beauty. Eastward the Alps reared up, serrating the horizon with a maze of glistening snow peaks. Seas of cloud filled the valleys, with innumerable dark, rocky pinnacles piercing through and giving the whole scene the appearance of a rock torn surf.

The air was keen edged and the cold was still severe, but after the icy blasts and the spear pointed showers of the previous day, the going was excellent. We were freed, too, from the anxiety of shaping our course by sheer navigation.

Nature's great map was no longer obscured. It lay unrolled below, an enlarged edition of our own tiny charts, on which we checked its features. Picking up the River Durance quite easily, we crossed it and passed above the city of Aix then swung east, heading for the coast and Cannes – across the famous Riviera.

Soon we caught sight of the sea. Five thousand feet below us the Mediterranean was laving the cliffs of innumerable little bays and

'Eastward the Alps reared up, serrating the horizon with a maze of glistening snow peaks ...'

inlets, embroidering a thin white edging of surf round their rugged bases – a narrow, white boundary line separating green-topped cliffs from deep-blue waters.

Then Nice lay below us. The city, with its fine buildings and avenues of palms, encircled by high hills, rests on the shores of a sea of wondrous blue. It is a place of ineffable charm and peace.

A large crowd had collected on the Promenade des Anglais to witness our flight and cheer us up. We flew low enough to distinguish the doll-like figures, and though we could not return their greetings we appreciated them none the less. Then onward again with a following breeze, white-cresting the blue sea that stretched away from beneath us to the southern horizon.

I knew there was an aerodrome at Pisa, since it was one of the stations on the air route to Egypt, so we decided to spend the night there and go on to Rome the next day.

Our flight toward Rome was one long battle against heavy headwinds and through dense clouds. We had been in the air barely an hour when the oil gauge on one of the engines dropped to zero.

Thinking that something had gone wrong with the lubricating system I switched off this engine and flew along close to the ground on the other engine, looking closely for a place to land. Fortunately we were not far from the Italian aerodrome at Venturina, and there I landed.

Sergeant Shiers quickly discovered that the fault was in the gauge itself, and not in the lubricating system, and it was only a matter of minutes before we were in the air again. The wind had increased and the rest of the voyage to Rome was boisterous and unpleasant.

Our average ground speed was a bare fifty miles an hour, so that it was not till late in the afternoon that we were above the city of the Caesars. In spite of the fatigue induced by our strenuous experiences of the day and our eagerness to get down to earth I could not help being stirred by the beauty of the historic city.

My original plan was to make the next stage a non-stop flight from Rome to Athens, thence to Cairo in another flight. This decision was the result of a report received in England that the aerodrome at Suda Ray, on the northern side of Crete, was flooded and would be unfit for landing till after winter.

The air attache at Rome, however, told us that the Suda Bay 'drome was still in good condition, but that I could make sure by dropping down at Taranto and inquiring at the British aerodrome there.

A glance at the map will show that the Cretan route saves a considerable distance, Suda Bay providing a halfway house. I therefore decided at once to take the Taranto course and try to save the long stretch of Mediterranean from Athens to Cairo.

After daylight, we left Rome in very bad weather. Our route for the first few miles followed the Appian Way, and as we were flying low we had a fine view of this ancient highway.

Our course now lay almost due east across the Apennines. Clouds had banked against the mountains and flying at times became extremely difficult owing to the bumpy nature of the atmosphere. Bumps of 400 and 500 feet, both upward and downward, were frequent.

Luckily a strong following wind was blowing and I was relieved when we got clear of the mountains and followed the coast down to Taranto, where we were greeted by officers of the RAF, Taranto being at that time a main stop on the London to Cairo route.

After a good night's rest in comfortable beds, we were up at our usual hour and made an early start for Suda Bay.

Once again the weather was cruel to us. First we flew east to the heel of Italy, and then headed across the open sea to the island of Corfu. Low clouds and rain forced us down to 800 feet above the sea.

The flight was miserable. The driving rain cut our faces and obscured all distant vision. Almost before we realised it, Corfu loomed up in the mist, and so I altered the course to southeast and flew down the coast of Greece.

The aerodrome at Suda Bay is rather a tricky place, being surrounded on three sides by high, rocky hills; but we succeeded in making a good landing.

On the morrow our longest oversea flight in this half of the voyage awaited us, so we spent the afternoon in a particularly thorough overhaul of the machine.

When we turned out next morning we found it had been raining heavily and the air was still thick with drizzle. The prospect was not good for crossing the island, which, though only a few miles wide, is intersected by an irregular range of mountains, of which the famous Mount Ida is one of the several peaks.

Nevertheless, we took off quite easily, and soon after leaving the ground encountered a layer of cloud, but pushed through and out – only to find ourselves beneath another stratum. Our charted route lay southeast, then south, with the southernmost point of the island as the objective, and I had been told that it was easy to follow a rough track leading from Canea through a pass in the mountains; but, with clouds above and below, it was not so easy.

I decided to try to locate the pass in the hope of getting through without the necessity of climbing above the mountains and so wasting valuable time. Fortune favoured us. I found the pass and to my joy discovered that there was just sufficient room for us to scrape over the top without entering the cloud.

We appeared to be only a few feet above the rocks when we cleared the crest, but it was preferable to having to barge blindly through the clouds, running the consequent risk of hitting a mountain crag.

On the southern side of the ranges the air was much clearer, and we were soon flying over the coastline. We took observations and set a compass course for Sollum, on the African coast. Two hundred and fifty miles of open sea had to be crossed.

Almost the last thing we had done before climbing aboard was to inflate the four spare inner tubes of our landing wheels; they would make first-class lifebuoys if we had to come down between Crete and Africa.

Our first glimpse of Africa was of a barren, desert coastline, but it was a welcome sight none the less, and we were not sorry to soon descry those landmarks of the ages, the Pyramids.

Before long we could pick out the minarets and mosques of the Egyptian capital itself. Now we were winging our way over Old Father Nile and across landmarks that were as familiar to me as the Heliopolis aerodrome itself, to which destination I was guiding the Vimy.

No wonder I glanced affectionately over the silent engines as we came to rest. I felt extremely happy as we sat there a moment or two, waiting for the fellows to come up and welcome us. We had come through from Suda Bay, a distance of 650 miles, in a non-stop flight of seven and a half hours, thus completing the first and worst of the four stages into which I had divided the total journey.

Part Four:
A Golden Sea of Desolation

We had intended staying a day in Cairo to rest but we were one day behind our scheduled time; so I decided that it must be made up.

We took off from Heliopolis aerodrome and for fifty miles followed the Ismailia Canal to Tel-el-Kebir. The banks were bordered by a patchwork of densely cultivated and irrigated lands; beyond, arid barrenness, sand, and nothing.

On the canal the great white lateen sails of dhows and feluccas in large numbers resembled a model yacht regatta. It was all very beautiful and wonderful.

Northward the waterways, canals and lakes of the Nile delta stood out like silver threads woven around the margins of patches in a quilt, for now the sun had burst through the clouds, and all the world sprang into life and light.

And soon to the straight cut of deep blue water that links north to south – the Suez Canal. Below, a P&O steamer is heading south. Perhaps she is bound for Australia and will call at Adelaide, my home and destination!

With a smile we contrasted the old and new methods if transportation and a throb of exultation filled us all. Still, we wondered, with unspoken thoughts, who would reach Australia first.

As we passed over Kantara, feelings of confidence filled me. We were now entering country I knew, having spent six months here with the Light Horse before I began flying. Furthermore, I had flown over the entire air route which now lay before us, as far as Java.

Kantara soon lay beyond the rolling eternity of sand. It was somewhere in these regions that the Children of Israel wandered for forty years. Forty minutes in the Vimy was quite sufficient for us. We looked down upon that golden sea of desolation, with only here and there a solitary clump of date palms, and we felt very sympathetic toward the Children of Israel!

Damascus offered a haven of rest. Great was our joy, on touching the ground, to be welcomed by old comrades and to be cared for. The Vimy, too, was looked after. Bennett and Shiers attended to their beloved engines, while I overhauled the controls and my brother filled up with fuel, ready for an early start on the morrow.

Imagine my dismay, on awakening next morning, to find heavy rain falling and the aerodrome surface rapidly becoming soft, with the wheels of the Vimy sinking in.

As there was no sign of the weather clearing up, we greased our tyres to assist their passage through the sticky clay and started up the engines. To my unspeakable relief, the Vimy moved ahead.

The takeoff was not lacking in excitement. The propellers sucked up water and mud which whirled in all directions, including ours. We rose into the air once more to be cut by the lash of the elements but, to my intense relief, the storm did not extend more than a few miles beyond Damascus.

On reaching Abu Kemal we turned southeast, following the course of the Euphrates. It was a pleasant change, after the interminable desert, to pursue the lazy course of the great river and to pass again over fertile tracts and numerous villages.

Soon we encountered strong headwinds, which diminished our speed considerably. I was becoming anxious as to whether we could reach Baghdad before dark, as I was not keen to make a night landing there. The sun was fast sinking in the west, and as we flew over Ramadie it dipped below the horizon. I decided that there would not be time to do the forty miles to Baghdad before dark. We selected a suitable landing ground among some old trenches, close to a cavalry camp, and landed.

We had landed on the old Ramadie battlefield, which was one of the notable sites of the Mesopotamian campaign. Soon after landing the C O of the Indian cavalry regiment came out to greet us, and proffered the hospitality of his camp.

We were delighted to learn there was a small supply of aviation petrol here, and we obtained sufficient to carry us through to Basra without having to land at Baghdad. An Indian guard was mounted over the machine, and the Vimy was securely lashed down for the night.

About 11 o'clock that night a heavy windstorm swooped down upon us, and my brother and myself rushed out to the machine. The wind had suddenly changed, and was now blowing hard on the tail of the machine. The Vimy was in imminent danger of being blown over and crashed.

We turned out fifty men from the nearest camp and they hung on to the machine until we started up the engines and swung her head round into the wind.

It was a pitch dark night, and the gale whirled the sand into blinding eddies, cutting our faces and eyes. One very severe gust caught one of the ailerons and snapped the top balance-wires. This allowed all four ailerons to flap about in a very dangerous manner, and it looked as though they would all he wrenched off before we could secure them.

By weight of arms, however, we eventually managed to secure the ailerons before serious damage was done. At last the machine was turned, facing the wind, and in that position successfully weathered the storm. Throughout the rest of the night the guard hung on to the machine and all stood by.

The storm abated by morning. We found that all the aileron control wires were strained or broken. The sand had choked up everything exposed to the weather, and by the time the damage had been repaired and our tanks filled with petrol it was noon.

For the first time since leaving London we had the promise of a good flying day with a following wind. This good fortune atoned for our troubles of the night and for our lack of sleep.

The flight to Basra took just under three hours and Basra we discovered to be a hive of activity. It was the main shipping port during the Mesopotamian campaign and the British military base and aerodrome extend for miles along the eastern bank.

As there was a Royal Air Force depot there, I decided to delay a day or two and allow Bennett and Shiers to overhaul and adjust the engines.

There was always plenty of work to be done at the end of each day's flying. Both of the engines had to be overhauled and cleaned, all parts of the machine examined and petrol and oil tanks refilled for the next journey. Usually this took us three or four hours every day.

We adopted a set program which we always carried out religiously. As soon as the machine landed Bennett and Shiers would don their overalls and set to work on the engines; the sparking plugs would be taken out and cleaned, magnetos examined and all parts of the engine inspected and cleaned. On this work to a large extent depended our success or failure.

Keith and I would climb out of our seats and talk to the people who had come out to meet us. Presently Keith would make enquiries about our petrol and oil supplies and get them brought up to the Vimy. I would then go off to the nearest post office and send our cables and get back to the Vimy as soon as I could. In addition, we had to run the gauntlet of functions and ceremonies, and it was difficult to make folk understand that work had to be done.

We deeply appreciated everyone's generous kindness, but I fear that on some occasions people must have thought us very discourteous.

By the time I returned to the machine Keith would have the petrol ready to put into the tanks and we would start work. This was very tiring and monotonous. I would open the four-gallon cans and lift them up to my brother, a distance of about six feet, and he would empty the cans into the tanks through a large funnel with a chamois leather strainer. Usually we lifted and filtered about half a ton of petrol into the machine and sometimes as much as a ton if we had just completed a long flight. I have always regarded this work as the hardest part of the whole flight.

We would land more or less tired after several hours in the air and then start on really hard work again. The temptation was always to let someone else do it and go off ourselves and rest, but other people might not have filtered the petrol properly, or done something wrong. We decided before we started that we would do all the work on the machine ourselves and as far as possible we carried this out.

By the time the tanks were full Bennett and Shiers would have the engines finished; we would then fill up the oil tanks with 'Castrol,' put the covers over the cockpit, and peg the machine down for the night. Putting in the 'Castrol' was always a messy job and we would usually finish our day's work very tired and very oily.

Fortunately we had foreseen all this and talked about it before we started; each man knew exactly what he had to do, and did it, and I think that anyone who has studied human nature will agree that, under these conditions it is a remarkable fact that never once was there a misunderstanding or a cross word spoken amongst our four selves.

On many occasions it was 9 or 10 pm before we left the machine for the night; we would then go off to either a hotel or some kind friend's house, bathe, dine, and in due course to bed. Each day we arose at 4.30 am and we never once had more than five hours sleep a night, usually it was about four, and then on through another similar day. Add to this the thrill, excitement, and strain of the whole race against time and one realizes that it is fortunate that we had gone into training and got ourselves very fit before leaving England.

On the morning of 23 November we left Basra for Bundar Abbas, 630 miles southeast.

Soon after starting the sun came up from the distant hills and the delicate shades of pink that flushed the horizon mounted higher and higher as another day of the flight began. The sunlight sparkled on our varnished wings and the polished propellers became halos of shimmering light. Our engines sang away merrily and the Vimy ceased to be a machine and pulsed with life, as if feeling the glory of the morning.

Bennett and Shiers, endeavouring to secure a well earned rest after their strenuous efforts of the past few days, were reclining inside the fuselage. As the spare parts were crammed into all the available space, however, theirs was a painful comfort indeed. The weather continued fine, the flight was mostly uninteresting and monotonous, and I brought the Vimy to a safe landing at Bundar Abbas where the British Consul, the Persian Governor, and a great concourse of interested locals gave us a hearty welcome.

Although dog tired, I could not sleep that night. The next day I hoped to reach Karachi in a non-stop flight of 730 miles. The distance did not perturb me in the least, but the treacherous, mountain scored country and the isolation from civilization, in case of a forced landing, was enough to give one a nightmare.

The British Consul had prepared an ostentatious looking document which commanded the local murderous tribes which infested the country to treat us kindly, in case we were forced to land among them!

Next day, however, Fortune favoured us once more with a following breeze and excellent weather and the country was merely a repetition of that passed over the previous day. For the last 100 miles we left the coast and flew on a compass bearing until we arrived at Karachi after a non-stop flight of eight and a half hours.

Our thoughts on this flight were often of Poulet, the French aviator who was somewhere ahead of us, and the first news that greeted us on landing at Karachi was that Poulet was at Delhi, only a day's flight in the lead! From now onward, added zest would be given to the flight.

We had hoped for a good rest at Karachi, but the local Royal Air Force officers had arranged a dinner and it was not until midnight that we went to bed. Three and a half hours later we were up ready for one of the longest non-stops we had undertaken, nine hours flying to Delhi, 720 miles away.

After circling the aerodrome we once more entered the monotony of landscape, pursuing the railway line for three hours across the dreary Sind Desert.

During the afternoon flying conditions became boisterous and turbulence tossed the Vimy around like a small vessel in a heavy sea. This was a welcome diversion for me as the past few days flying had cramped me in one position and I was now kept active and on the move keeping the machine straight and fighting the air pockets and bumps into which we plunged and fell.

We first noticed Delhi from fifty miles away, a white streak in a haze of green plain. We had established a record by arriving thirteen days after leaving London and we were welcomed by General McEwan, the Royal Air Force chief in India and many old friends.

I regretted that I was unable to reply to their kindly expressions of welcome, as I did not hear them. The roar of the exhausts for nine hours had made me quite deaf. It was several hours before my hearing returned and, when it did, I learned that Poulet had left that morning for Allahabad.

We were desperately in need of rest after several strenuous days flying, but we took our rest in the form of the proverbial change of jobs and spent six hours working on the machine to make everything ready for an early start next day.

Half the journey was completed and Poulet was within range.

PART FIVE:
AN EAGLE AND A SPARROW

At 4.30 am next day I tumbled very stiffly out of bed on the insistence of an alarm clock. Oh, for another day off! But by the time the others had uncoiled and emerged into the early Indian dawn, I felt again the keenness of the chase.

And so into the air once more, and on to Agra – the city of the Taj Mahal.

Of all the remembered scenes wonderful and beautiful, that of the Taj Mahal remains the most vivid and the most exquisite. There it lay below us, dazzling in the strong sunlight – a vision in marble. Seen from the ground, one's emotions are stirred by the extraordinary delicacy of its workmanship. Viewed from 3000 feet above, the greater part of its infinite detail is lost, but one sees it as a whole. It lies like a perfectly executed miniature or a matchless white jewel reclining in a setting of Nature's emeralds.

We hovered lazily around, exposed our photographic plates, and swung off on our course. In the vastness of space through which we were speeding, the magnificent monument became a toy . . . a mote . . . a memory.

New scenes, villages, and towns rose from the unreachable brink ahead, grew into being, passed beneath, then out over the brim of the world behind us.

We were crossing the vast plains of Central India, a great flat tessellation of cultivated patches that gave an impression of the earth being covered with green, brown, and golden tiles. These multi-tinted patches were framed with brimming channels carrying the irrigation waters from the great river.

Allahabad was reached after four and a half hours, and we eagerly but vainly searched the aerodrome for a glimpse of Poulet. There were several hangars on the aerodrome and we thought that his machine might be under cover, but on landing we were informed that he had left that same morning for Calcutta.

It was too late to continue the chase that afternoon, but next morning saw us early on the wing. Once more pursuing the course of the Jumna as far as Benares, we headed southeast and followed the railroad to Calcutta.

Thousands of people had collected on the racecourse, at the far side of the city, to witness our arrival, and when we landed it was with great difficulty that the police kept back the multitude that surged around the machine. A barrier was at last placed around the Vimy and soon we became the centre of a compact mass of peering faces, all struggling to get closer and obtain a better view. The elusive Poulet, we learned, had moved off the same morning for Akyab.

That night, after the usual overhaul of engines and filling up with petrol, we stayed with friends and slept well. We had crossed India and were now more than halfway to Australia.

Our departure next morning from Calcutta was marked by an incident that might easily have spelled disaster to us. The racecourse is really too small for a machine as large as our Vimy to manoeuvre with safety and I was a trifle nervous about the takeoff; but the surface was good, our engines in fine trim, and she rose like a bird.

Then came our narrow escape. A large number of kite hawks were flying around, alarmed by the size and noise of this new great bird in their midst. When we had cleared the ground by about ten feet two hawks flew across us at an angle; they seemed to become confused and turned straight into us, one striking the wing and the other flying straight into the port propeller. There was a crash as if a stone had hit the blade, and then a scatter of feathers.

It may not sound very dreadful – except for the hawk – but as a matter of fact it was a breathless, not to say a terrifying moment, for we fully expected to hear the crash of broken propeller blades. We were at the time flying straight for the high trees, and, had the propeller broken, nothing could have saved us from a terrible crash.

More hawks were circling about, and in endeavouring to avoid them I almost crashed the machine on the treetops and I was deeply relieved when we had climbed to 1000 feet and were clear of the pestilent birds.

I marvelled that our propeller stood the impact, for a very trifling knock will cause the disruption of a propeller when running "full out," and so in an extremely high state of tension. (I have known so tiny an object as a cigarette end thrown carelessly into a propeller to cause the whirling blades to fly to pieces!)

On looking over the machine I noticed one of the hawk's wings had become pinned in the rigging, and we secured it after the day's flight as a souvenir of a hairbreadth escape.

Calcutta marked the completion of the second stage of our journey, and from now onward the route would be much more difficult and hazardous. We had had the benefit of RAF aerodromes and personnel at almost every landing place, but henceforth we would have to land on racecourses, or very small aerodromes. Also, I knew that the only possible landing places right on to Port Darwin were at stated places hundreds of miles apart, and that in the event of engine trouble our chances of making a safe forced landing were very slender.

I had originally intended flying from Calcutta to Rangoon racecourse in one flight, but as the next day, November 29th, was a Saturday, and a race meeting would he held at Rangoon on that day, I decided to stop at Akyab.

My brother peered over the side as we circled above the aerodrome and showed symptoms of great excitement, while Bennett and Shiers waved joyfully from their cockpit and pointed down to the ground. They indicated a small machine near the centre of the field. It was Poulet!

Poulet was the first to greet us on landing. He came forward with a cheery smile and outstretched hand – a true sportsman, the hero of a gallant and daring enterprise. I was deeply interested in inspecting Poulet's machine, which was drawn up alongside the Vimy.

In proportion the contrast was reminiscent of an eagle and a sparrow. The Vimy towered above the tiny Caudron, which appeared altogether too frail and quite unsuited for the hazardous task these two courageous fellows had embarked upon.

I had a long talk with Poulet and his mechanic, Benoist, and we agreed to fly on together the next day to Rangoon, but when morning arrived, as we still had some work to complete on the machine, Poulet set off, and by the time we were ready he had an hour's lead.

No aeroplane had ever landed at Rangoon before, and naturally I was very keen to win the honour for the Vimy. For the first 100 miles I followed the coastline southward and did not observe a single landing place in case of necessity.

Flying east, we crossed a low mountain chain, and on the other side found the Irrawaddy River. We followed down its course as far as Prome. From here the railroad guided us on to Rangoon. I had no difficulty in locating the racecourse, it was a green patch framed by a compact ring of cheering humanity.

We came to earth midst tempestuous cheering, and were welcomed by the Lieutenant-Governor of Burma. We were told that no race meeting had been so well attended as the present, nor had the betting been so widespread. The multitudes had massed to witness two aeroplanes racing halfway across the globe. To them the race was more than novel; it was a great event in their lives, for few indeed of the vast assemblage had ever seen an aeroplane.

As flying conditions from Akyab had been boisterous, we in our high-powered machine had a great advantage over Poulet and in spite of the hour's handicap at the outset, we succeeded in reaching Rangoon an hour ahead of him.

Poulet's arrival was the signal for another outburst of cheering, and he was welcomed no less warmly than ourselves.

We had arranged with Poulet to start off together next morning and keep company as far as Bangkok.

A great crowd swarmed over the aerodrome, and the police and troops were clearing them off prior to our departure. We started up the engines, took leave of our kind friends, and waited, but Poulet had some difficulty with his machine. It was a warm morning and our engines were beginning to get hot, so I took off and circled above the racecourse for twenty minutes; but, as Poulet had not yet left the ground, I concluded that he must be experiencing engine trouble, and so reluctantly we had to push off without him.

The maps we carried of this country were very poor and sadly lacking in detail, but they indicated that a 7000 foot mountain range had to be crossed before reaching Bangkok.

We flew southeast over country rapidly becoming mountainous; but, instead of encountering lofty summits, a mighty cloud bank, that seemed to reach to heaven and bar the entire prospect in the direction of our course extended before us. The monsoon season was now due, and I concluded that this would be one of the initial storms.

Somewhere in that dread barrier lay the high peaks over which we must cross, and I admit that I was afraid of the prospect.

As time wore on, the storms would grow in frequency and intensity, so I decided to plunge ahead.

The clouds rested down to 4000 feet, and we were flying just beneath them. Somewhere ahead lay summits another 3000 feet higher. Our maps indicated a pass which we tried to find, and so we started off along a deep valley.

At first it looked hopeful, but after five minutes' flying the cliffs narrowed in, and, fearing I might be trapped in a tapering dead end, I turned the Vimy about. There was just sufficient room in which to effect the manoeuvre.

It seemed that our safest course was to climb above the cloud mass or at least to an altitude sufficiently high to clear the mountain tops, and barge our way through the mist. At 9000 feet we emerged above the first layer; but eastward the clouds appeared to terrace up gradually, and in the distance there extended still another great wall, towering several thousand feet higher.

Before starting off over this sea of clouds, my brother took observations with the drift indicator, and we found to our dismay that we would have to fight into a twenty-mile-an-hour headwind. He gave me the compass bearing to fly on, and away we went once more, with the world lost to view beneath us.

The map showed the range to be about fifty miles wide, and after we had flown for half an hour, still another cloud barrier appeared directly ahead.

Our machine had now reached its 'ceiling', so there was no alternative but to plunge ahead into the mist. We were then flying at an altitude of 11 000 feet and were soon engulfed in a dense blanket of mist.

As we had left England hurriedly, there had been no time to fit special cloud navigation instruments, and the only ones we carried for this purpose were the ordinary compass, air speed indicator and inclinometer.

Down below us lay jagged mountain peaks buried by cloud. Ahead, around, and behind, the mist enfolded us in an impenetrable screen, and if I once allowed the machine to get beyond control, a horrible fate would be waiting for us all below.

The moment one plunges into heavy cloud there is misty blankness; all objects are lost to view; and as time wears on, a helpless feeling grows upon one that all sense of direction is lost. To overcome this predicament, I settled down to try to watch all three of the aforementioned instruments and maintain their readings correctly. In addition it was necessary to glance over the engines and the gauges continually.

After an hour of these tense and nerve-racking conditions both Keith and I concluded that we must surely be across the mountain range. So I decided to take the risk and go lower and 'feel'.

Shutting off both engines, we glided down, and I held up the machine so that we were going as slowly as possible – only about forty miles an hour.

As we approached the 7000-foot level, which I knew to be the height of the range, we huddled together and held on tight, in anticipation of the crash!

By the time we reached 4000 feet, I concluded that the range had been crossed and a few minutes later we burst out into full view of a glorious world, carpeted with trees, 1500 feet below. The sudden transformation was stunning. It was an unspeakable relief – the end of an hour that was one of the worst nightmare experiences I have ever passed through.

Before our bewildered gaze there stretched a dark-green forest, only limited by the distant skyline. Here and there the dark green was splashed with patches of bright coloured creeper, and in spite of the fact that there was not the vestige of a possible landing place, it was beautiful and a welcome relief. Later, the Siamese told us that all this country was unexplored.

An hour later and we reached the Mekon River and the haunts of man. Following downstream, we landed at Don Muang aerodrome, twelve miles north of Bangkok, after a flight that will live long in my memory. Don Muang is the headquarters of the Siamese Flying Corps. They have several hangars, a number of machines, and up-to-date workshops. During my visit to Siam the previous year I had been to Don Muang, so that on landing I found myself among friends.

Part Six:
Emeralds in Settings of Torquoise

My original plan was to fly from Bangkok to Singapore, roughly 1000 miles, in one flight; but as I learned there was a good aerodrome at Singora, about halfway, with 500 gallons of petrol depoted there, and as I was anxious to conserve the machine as much as possible, I decided to land at the latter place.

We left Bangkok in good weather, and were escorted for the first hour. The flying conditions were ideal with a good following wind; then ahead again lay our old enemies the clouds. At this time we were flying along the coast, so did not deem it necessary to climb above them. The clouds became lower and heavier and soon we found ourselves only 1000 feet above the sea.

Ahead we saw the rain, and I dreaded what was to come. While we were over the sea, with the land on our right, there was comparatively little chance of our crashing into anything. This was fortunate, for in a few moments we were soaked through, our goggles became saturated, and all vision for more than a few hundred yards or so was obliterated. The rain came down literally like a sheet of water, and as we had to remove our goggles and maintain a constant lookout ahead, we were almost blinded by the rain lashing our unprotected eyes.

At this time we were doing ninety miles per hour, and as the torrential rain dashed against us and the machine it smote like hail. Narrowing my eyes down to slits, I peered out ahead as long as I could endure it; that was but a few minutes. I then tapped Keith to keep the watch while I rested my eyes; then, when he could see no more, I would 'carry on' again. So it went on for the best part of three hours.

As long as we were flying south; the strong wind helped us; but as we had to follow the coastline in detail, and there were many bays and headlands we frequently found ourselves fighting right into the teeth of the gale to get out of a bay or around a headland.

I was afraid to go inland, as the rain only allowed us limited visibility. Once we almost crashed on to a hill, which suddenly loomed up through the rain ahead. I just had time, by a hair's breadth. to pull the machine around in a climbing turn and go farther out to sea. I have never experienced worse flying conditions, and had it been at all possible to land, I gladly would have done so.

At last we reached Singora, and a glance at the aerodrome showed that at least half of it was underwater. There was, however, a narrow strip along the centre which appeared more or less dry, but I would have to make a landing across wind. I came down low to examine this strip, and to my utter dismay noticed that it was covered with small tree stumps!

A wide and anxious circling around the aerodrome showed me there was no other spot on which to land; so there was nothing for it but to attempt to make a landing on this narrow strip of stump-studded ground.

As we touched and ran along, I expected every moment to feel a jolt and the undercarriage wrenched off, or else the machine thrown on to her nose; but by the merciful guidance of Providence we miraculously came to rest safely.

The only damage sustained was to our tail skid, which had caught in a stump and been wrenched off. I walked back along our tracks and found that in several instances our wheels had missed by a few inches stumps a foot to eighteen inches high.

My first inquiry was as to the quantity of petrol available. I discovered that the supposed 500 gallons was only 500 litres, depoted there for Poulet.

This meant we would be compelled to remain here until I could get sufficient petrol from Penang or Bangkok to take us on to Singapore. I accordingly sent off an urgent wire to the Asiatic Petroleum Company at Penang asking them to send me 200 gallons of aviation petrol as speedily as possible.

I next requested the Governor of Singora to have part of the aerodrome cleared of stumps to enable us to take off.

Our machine was left standing on the strip of high ground and we pegged her down securely for the night.

Our next job was to mend the tail skid.

We found a local, a jack of all trades and the master of a promising heap of scrap iron. Bennett unearthed a piece of steel shafting which he shaped by the light of a kerosene lamp on a lathe powered by four men turning a large pulley wheel, at a nearby rice mill.

After breakfast we returned to the machine, fitted the new tail-skid, and found that the governor had sent down 200 local convicts from the local jail to clear away the stumps. We set them to work clearing a strip about 400 yards long and fifty yards wide across the aerodrome.

The day's rest was not only a delightful relaxation, it was an imperative necessity as my own and my brother's eyes were almost too painful for vision after the battle with the storm the previous day.

Late that afternoon our petrol arrived from Penang, but it was raining too heavily to risk putting it into the machine.

We were down at the aerodrome at daylight putting the petrol into the tanks. Getting the machine into the air was a questionable problem but our time for reaching Australia was fast closing in, so we decided to make the attempt.

Three large patches of water extended across the aerodrome at intervals of about fifty yards. This water was, on average, about six inches deep but, as the soil was sandy, our wheels did not sink into it appreciably.

The first water almost pulled us up. By the time we passed through the second patch we were moving scarcely any faster than when we began. By the third pool we were travelling about thirty miles per hour and the sudden impact with the water almost threw the Vimy on her nose as water was sucked up and thrown everywhere by the propellers.

We had now just seventy yards of dry ground remaining on which to gain flying speed, and beyond that extended scrub and gorse bushes.

The Vimy bounded forward as soon as we left the water and just managed to get sufficient lift to clear a ditch and scrape over the scrub. We then followed the railway line, crossed to the western side of the peninsular, and flew over tin mines and rubber plantations, past Kuala Lumpur, and on down to Singapore.

I had been dreading landing and taking off at Singapore as the improvised aerodrome at the racecourse was altogether too small for our aircraft. I glided the Vimy down at as low a speed as possible and, just before we touched the ground, Bennett clambered from the cockpit and slid down the fuselage to the tailplane. His weight dropped the tail quickly and the machine pulled up in about one hundred yards after touching the ground.

The heat in Singapore was intense and, coming from a cold English winter, we felt it severely. It was already getting hot at daylight next morning when my brother and I examined the ground and discussed the best way to take off. We were both very dubious as to whether we would get the machine into the air or pile her into the adjacent houses. The ground was much too small for an aerodrome and overnight rain had made it very heavy.

I taxied into the position we had decided was best, opened the throttle full out, and watched the fence around the course come rapidly nearer and nearer.

It was a tense and anxious moment when I pulled my control lever back fifty yards from the fence, but the trusty Vimy cleared the rails and rose steeply so her wheels and undercarriage just cleared the treetops and rooftops. She achieved the seemingly impossible and, to this day, I regard our escape from disaster during that perilous takeoff to be providential!

After a wide sweep above Singapore we headed for the open sea and Java.

Passing down the Sumatran coast we ran into typical doldrums weather, isolated patches of dark thunderclouds from which the rain teemed in heavy murky columns. Occasional forks of lightning seared the clouds, throwing their dark bulk into relief and shedding a flickering gleam over the calm sea.

On crossing the coast we encountered a headwind and bumpy conditions and one immense vacuum into which we fell made us hold tight.

'That's the equator!' exclaimed my brother, and, sure enough, our dead reckoning told us we had just bumped across the line.

Our entry into the southern hemisphere was met with improved weather, but the landscape below was dense jungle, fringed along the seashore by mangrove swamps and the blue tropical sea. This kindled in my mind thoughts of utter helplessness in case of engine trouble.

I had originally intended to hug the coast of Sumatra on to Java. As the landscape was all dense mangrove swamp with no sign of a landing place, however, I reasoned we might as well fly over the sea and my brother computed a compass course for Batavia.

As the mountains marking the end of Java began to show up on the starboard, a scene of rare enchantment began to resolve itself on the glorious mirror of the sea.

Numerous small islets, emeralds in settings of turquoise, were passing beneath us. The Thousand Islands, each one beautiful, fringed with a ribbon of beach and set in an exquisite green, then deep blue, combined to make one of the most beautiful sights I have ever looked down upon. Myriads of tiny white fisher sails passed through the channels, gleaning a harvest from the sea.

Reluctantly, we turned from this glimpse of fairyland and soon reached Batavia, city of canals and beautiful avenues. Here we were treated with the greatest hospitality and kindness and the governor gave orders that we were to be the guests of his government while passing through the Dutch East Indies.

I was delighted to learn that several aerodromes had been constructed for our use between Java and Australia. I thanked his

'... the unsurpassable beauty that unfolded below, a vast bounteous garden ...'
The Vimy over Java.

Excellency for his kindness and interest in our flight, without which we would never have reached Australia within the allotted thirty days.

The petrol available here was very heavy and it took us six hours to strain 350 gallons through a chamois leather strainer into the tanks. As the next stage to Surabaya was a short lap, time was not a real concern and we left at 7.30 am with beautiful weather favouring us and sped rapidly over fertile tracts of this amazing island, charmed by the unsurpassable beauty that unfolded below, a vast bounteous garden with immense, shapely volcanic cones.

PART SEVEN:
A PATHWAY OF BAMBOO MATS

Nearing Surabaya, flying became very bumpy, and it was no small relief when the town, like a magic carpet of multi coloured fabric, spread beneath us. Heading the Vimy down, we made a low circle above the town, to the amazement of the population that swarmed out into the streets, petrified, evidently, by the visitation.

From above, the surface of the aerodrome on which we were to land appeared to be ideal, but the whole ground was small. I landed along the south side intending to open up one engine and swing the machine round on the ground if there appeared any danger of overshooting and running into a bank of earth at the end. We made a good landing and were easing off to rest when the machine seemed to drag, and from past experience I knew at once the Vimy was becoming bogged.

Opening up the starboard engine, we began to swing slowly, but the port wheels immediately sank into the mud and we tilted on to our fore skid. At once I shut off both engines and the Vimy gradually eased back to her normal position. I then discovered that our aerodrome was a stretch of land that had been reclaimed from the sea; the top crust had set quite hard, but underneath was a layer of liquid mud.

The people, who had been kept back by the Dutch soldiers, rushed the ground, and their weight on the sun-dried crust soon broke it up, and mud began to ooze through. In a very short while the Vimy subsided to her axles and was surrounded by a pond of semi-liquid mud.

The proposition literally was a decidedly sticky one. It was midday, broiling hot, and the tenacity of the mud reminded me forcibly of that clinging tendency familiar to our black soil plains. Moreover, only four days of our prescribed time remained in which we must make Port Darwin.

The engineer of the Harbour Board arrived, and together we discussed the situation. He collected a horde of labourers and a large quantity of bamboo matting, and we set to work to dig out the wheels. After some hard work we got the matting almost under the wheels, started up the engines and aided by the labourers and Dutch soldiers, the Vimy was hauled from the bog. I then stopped the engines, tied ropes to the undercarriage, and the machine was hauled on to a pathway of mats.

The machine was safely out of the morass, and the ground on which we stood felt quite solid so I thought we had landed on the only soft spot on the aerodrome and decided to taxi to the opposite end under our own engine power.

After ten yards, down went the wheels again. More digging, tugging, and pushing, and we, apprehensive all the while as to whether the workers would drag off the undercarriage, finally had to lay down a pathway of bamboo mats and have the machine hauled by 200 men.

We had landed at 12 noon and after six hours of hard work under a boiling tropical sun we had the Vimy on a platform of bamboo mats at the end of the aerodrome. Some of the matting had large nails sticking out of it and two of our tyres were punctured. Bennett and Shiers as usual attended the engines first, while Keith and I replenished our tanks with petrol and oil. Fortunately we didn't have to put in as much petrol as usual. We then attacked the two punctured tyres. By this time it was dark, but we worked on by the light from the lamps of a motorcar.

Fully loaded, the Vimy weighs about six tons, and just as we had got one wheel jacked up the ground beneath sank under the weight and the jack broke. We borrowed another jack, but this suffered a similar fate. We had had no food since early morning so disconsolate we decided to leave the machine for the night and resume our efforts in the morning. I don't think I have ever felt so tired or so miserable in my life as I did then. Here we were only 1200 miles from Australia; we still had four of our thirty days left in which to do it, and yet to all intents and purposes we were hopelessly stuck in this quagmire without a chance of getting out of it.

Furthermore, I knew that this was the only flat stretch of land within 400 miles from which it was possible to get the Vimy into the air. It seemed as if victory were to be snatched from us at the last moment.

But just when things were looking blackest my brother had a bright idea. Why not construct a roadway of mats to prevent our wheels sinking into the mud?

We found the Harbour Board engineer but he said it would be impossible to get so many mats together in so short a time. After much persuasion he agreed to have as many mats as possible at the aerodrome next morning. This cheering news considerably revived our sinking spirits and we went off to our hotel in a much happier frame of mind.

Next morning saw us at the aerodrome by daylight, and a gladsome sight met our eyes. Locals were streaming in from every direction bearing sheets of bamboo matting – they were literally carrying their houses on their backs – and already a great pile of it lay by the Vimy.

At first a pathway of mats was merely laid down, but in our keen anxiety to set off we had overlooked the 'slipstream' from the propellers. The engines were opened up and we were just gathering speed nicely when some of the sheets were whisked up and blown into the tailplane. This threw the machine out of control and to our dismay the Vimy ran off the matting and

14,000 Miles Through the Air Ross Smith

'Once more we had to dig deep down and place great planks under the wheels.'

14,000 Miles Through the Air Ross Smith

'More matting arrived ... so we made the road about 300 yards long and 40 feet wide ...'

bogged again. Once more we had to dig deep down and place great planks under the wheels and haul the Vimy back into the matting. I have never been able to understand how the machine stood the rough handling she received; it speaks volumes for the material and thoroughness of her construction.

More matting arrived on a motor lorry, so we made the road about 300 yards long and 40 feet wide and this time pegged it all down and interlaced the mats so that they couldn't blow up. At last all was ready and just 24 hours after our arrival at Surabaya we started up the engines, ran along the roadway and with feelings of intense relief felt the Vimy take off.

We circled low over the town and anchorage, so as to give the engines time to settle down to normal running and then headed on a direct compass course for Bima.

From the point of view of a prospective forced landing, the 400-mile flight to Bima was impossible. Not a single flat occurred on which we might have landed. Scenically, this lap was glorious. We skirted the coast of Bali and Lombok, keeping 3000 feet above the sea. Not a ripple disturbed its surface and looking over the side from time to time I could see a lot of small splashes in the water in the form of a circle. For a time these splashes puzzled me and then I caught a glint of silvery wings and knew that they were made by flying fish. My brother also had seen them and we were both able to see flying fish from a height of 3000 feet. It made me think that perhaps after all the hawks and other birds that we see flying about have not such wonderful eyesight as we imagine, because it is undoubtedly easier to see an object from the air than on the ground.

Bima aerodrome in the island of Sumbawa was in excellent condition and clearly marked with a huge white cross in the centre which we saw several miles away.

The local Sultan and the Dutch commissioner met us and proffered the hospitality of a bungalow a couple of miles from the machine.

The next morning locals were swarming around the machine with presents of coconuts sufficient to start a plantation; they must have thought the Vimy a very thirsty sort of bird.

We took a cargo of nuts on board, as the water was unsuited for drinking, and set off in dazzling sunshine, following the north coast of Flores to Reo. On the south side of the island we ran into isolated rainstorms. Once we saw a small active volcano in the distance and were tempted to go off and gaze down into its smoking crater, but as the weather indicated a change for the worse, we could not afford to deviate. We flew on as far as Pandar, then swung off direct for Timor.

We had by this time acquired such confidence in our engines that it mattered little whether sea or land lay below us.

A thick haze obscured the land and all distant vision, but we eventually picked up the Timor coast a few hundred yards from our calculated position. Ten miles inland we came down on the aerodrome at Atamboea, our last landing ground before Port Darwin, where Dutch officials had thoughtfully arranged our petrol and oil supply close at hand, saving us a good deal of valuable time, which we devoted to a thorough overhaul.

Tomorrow would be the great day whereupon reposed the destiny of our hopes, labours, and ideals. This was one of the aerodromes specially made by the Governor-General of the Netherlands Indies for the Australian flight, and had been completed only the day before our arrival. A guard of Dutch soldiers kept watch over the machine while we proceeded with their officers to camp, some six miles away.

PART EIGHT:
'HERE GOES!'

None of us overslept. We were too excited. We felt sure that if tomorrow dawned fine and hot, our homing was assured; but as we stepped out, before sunrise, into the still, sluggish air, we realized our hopes of an early start were small. A heavy haze lay over the sea and coast, obscuring everything.

We were at the aerodrome before sunup to discover that a crowd of locals were even earlier risers than ourselves. Most had come on foot, but many had ridden their ponies, and they clustered around the fence, behind and beside the Vimy like swarming bees. We hauled the machine well back with the tail against the fence to take advantage of every foot of the short run.

If an aeroplane is forced to land in the sea it usually floats for a time, then the forward part sinks and only the tail remains above water. Remembering this, just before leaving Timor we tied a parcel of food, a bottle of water, the pistol and some cartridges on to the tail so that we would have something to fall back upon in case of emergency.

Soon after 8 am the fog began to thin, and at 8.35, to be exact, I opened up the engines and just managed to scrape out of the 'drome. Scrape is exactly the word, for the branch-tops of the gum trees rasped along the bottom of the machine as we rose. It was one of the closest shaves of the trip.

In front of us rose a chain of high hills. As the atmosphere was hot, we climbed very slowly and made a detour to avoid them.

Still flying low, we approached the coast and pulled ourselves together for the final lap – the jump across the Arafura Sea that lay between us and Port Darwin.

Keith took all possible bearings, noted wind direction, and made numerous calculations of ground speeds. Then we set compass course for Darwin and with a 'Here goes!' we were out over the sea. All our hearts were beating a little quicker; even our fine old engines seemed to throb a trifle faster.

This was to be our longest stretch over open sea and I did not relish the prospect of being out of sight of land for five hours. However, as the coastline of Timor receded and disappeared behind us, I remembered the great trans-Atlantic flight made by the late Sir John Alcock in a Vimy similar to our own. What had we to fear with only a few hundred miles of open sea to cross, when he had nearly 2000?

The Australian Government had arranged that a warship should patrol the sea between Timor and Port Darwin in case we should

14,000 Miles Through the Air Ross Smith

'We swooped low and ... passed over the vessel.' HMAS Sydney photographed by Ross Smith.

need help, and anxiously we scanned the distant horizon for the first glimpse of her.

Our watches registered 11.48 when Keith nodded ahead and dead on the line of flight we made out a faint smoke that soon resolved itself into the smoke plume of a fighting-ship. It was the HMAS *Sydney* and we knew now that, whatever might befall, we had a friend at hand.

We swooped low, and exactly at twelve minutes past noon passed over the vessel, seeing plainly the upturned faces of the sailors and their waving hands. It was a cheer of welcome quite different from anything that we had experienced on the long journey. Perhaps it is not to be wondered at that the result of our snapshot was blurred through the shaking of the camera.

We took the opportunity of snatching a speed test and found we were averaging seventy-five miles an hour.

Two hours later both of us saw ahead and to port what appeared to be haze, but which we hoped was land, though neither dared express his hopes. They were justified, however, ten minutes later, and, hailing Bennett and Shiers, we pointed joyfully to Bathurst Island lighthouse.

It was just 2.06 pm when, as our diary prosaically notes, we 'observed Australia'. At 3 o'clock we not only observed it, but rested firmly upon it, for, having circled over Darwin and come low enough to observe the crowds and the landing place, we landed on Terra Australis on December 10th, 27 days, 20 hours after taking off from Hounslow.

We had won the race against time and the £10 000 prize with just 52 hours to spare!

Two zealous customs and health officials were anxious to examine us, but so were about 2000 just ordinary citizens, and the odds of 1000 to 1 were rather long for those departmental men, and our welcome was not delayed.

The hardships and perils of the past month were forgotten in the excitement of the present. We shook hands with one another, our hearts swelling with those emotions invoked by achievement and the glamour of the moment. It was, and will be, perhaps, the supreme hour of our lives.

Almost reverently we looked over the Vimy and unspoken admiration crept over us as we paid a silent tribute to those in far off England for their sterling and honest craftsmanship. The successful issue of the venture in a great degree was due to them, and surely they merited and deserved a large proportion of the praise.

The Vimy had passed through every possible climatic rigour and not once, from the time we took our departure from Hounslow, had she ever been under shelter. I looked over her, aglow with pride, the Vimy loomed up as the zenith of man's inventive and constructional genius. I could find neither fault nor flaw in the construction, and, given a few days' overhaul on the engines, the Vimy would have been quite capable of turning round and flying back to England.

These reflections were brief, for the crowd, having satisfied its curiosity over the machine, directed it to us. The Administrator of the Northern Territory and the Mayor of Darwin were given barely time to make an official welcome when the assemblage, brimming with enthusiasm, lifted us shoulder high and conveyed us to the jail.

This gave us qualms and we fully expected a charge of exceeding the speed limit to be brought against us. Our apprehension dissolved as we were dumped on a tree stump, historic or otherwise, in the garden, while raucous howls of 'Speech! Speech!' came from the hospitable multitude.

After the exchange of much 'hot air' on both sides, we returned to the Vimy, made all snug, and lashed her down for the night.

And now we were to be bewildered by an amazing array of cables and telegrams. They arrived in great fifteen-minute shoals from every corner of the globe.

What had gone wrong? Surely everyone had gone mad – or had we? Why all this fuss and excitement?

Since leaving London we had not read a newspaper, and, beyond the local natural attention evinced at our numerous landing grounds, we knew nothing of the interest the rest of the work was taking in the flight.

Great indeed was our astonishment when in back files of newspapers, we read of our exploits, recorded with a degree of detail that must have taxed the imaginative resources of editorial staffs.

PART NINE:
THE LONG WAY HOME

The rush, strain, and anxiety were over; henceforward the conclusion of our flight across Australia could be undertaken leisurely, but we still had a distance of 3000 miles to fly before reaching our home in Adelaide.

Our flying time from London to Darwin was 135 hours. We should have given our engines a top overhaul – lifted the cylinders and ground in the valves, etc. This would have taken a week, and as the rainy season had just started and our aerodrome was low-lying, I was told that if we did not get off at once we would probably have to remain three months.

The port propeller was showing signs of splitting but I thought it would last until we reached Sydney where we could get another. All things considered I thought it best to get on as quickly as possible, because standing out in the open in Darwin the Vimy risked being severely damaged in one of the frequent tropical storms.

The Minister of Defence at Melbourne had arranged petrol and oil supplies for us at various points and the first town we would reach after leaving Port Darwin was Cloncurry, in Northwestern Queensland – a distance of about 1000 miles. The maps of all that northern part of Australia are bad and show very little detail, but we arranged to get some information about various landmarks from some stockmen who had recently returned from 'droving' a mob of cattle from Darwin to Cloncurry.

Our first mechanical troubles of the whole journey began soon after leaving Darwin.

We were following the telegraph line which runs overland from Darwin to Adelaide; it was terribly hot and below us stretched a limitless expanse of undulating scrub country. After about four hours of very uncomfortable flying, valve trouble developed in the starboard engine and I decided to land on a dried-up swamp a few miles ahead. It turned out to be very rough ground, but we got down safely and Shiers soon had the engine right again.

There was a good waterhole at one side of the swamp and as flying conditions were so bad we decided to lay up under the shade of the wings for the rest of the day and go on early next morning. We learned afterward that the place where we had landed rejoices in the name of 'Warlock Ponds,' and I am never likely to forget it as long as I live.

As soon as the sun went down a solitary mosquito came buzzing around our little camp and presently selected Shiers as his victim. Finding him good, the mosquito, being a sportsman, did not wait until he had had his fill, but buzzed off back to his pals at the waterhole and told them of his find. In a few minutes the air was thick with them and I have never known insects so venomous.

Sleep was impossible and the only way we could rest was by wrapping ourselves completely in a blanket, but it was too hot to do this for long. We tried grass fires, a petrol fire, and everything else that we could think of, but all to no avail, and soon our faces, arms, and legs were just a mass of lumps.

About midnight I suddenly remembered that I had a bottle of very good Irish whisky in the machine that had been given me in London. It had not been opened and so at last I thought I had found something to keep these pests away. The whisky was divided into four portions and at once I proceeded to splash mine all over myself while the others watched the result. It was not long in coming. I am sure those mosquitoes must have thought it was Christmas; they fairly swarmed around me and then kept coming back for another drink!

To add to my discomfort I was forced to watch Keith and Bennett and Shiers drink their portions while I vainly tried to lick up the drips that were running down my face.

It was after daylight before we managed to sleep and so our start was delayed until 10 am. If anything it was hotter than the preceding day and consequently the air was full of pockets and bumps and at times I had to work hard to keep the machine under control.

We left the telegraph line at Newcastle Waters and turned off southeast. There was nothing on our map to guide us, but the stockmen in Port Darwin told us that if we flew southeast from Newcastle Waters for about 100 miles we would see two large patches of scrub which almost met each other in the form of a V. Then if we went down low, we would see the tracks of a mob of cattle that they had driven over there a few months previously. A few miles further on we would come onto a rough bush road that led on toward Cloncurry.

It all came out just as they had said; we picked out the two patches of scrub and then came down and saw the tracks of the cattle.

Surely this was rather a novel form of navigation.

About an hour later I was startled by a loud crack from the port propeller and was horrified to see that one blade had split from the tip to the boss. There was a tent pitched by the side of a track about a mile ahead, so I shut off both engines and came down and landed.

We calculated that we were about twenty miles away from Anthony's Lagoon where there was a small police station and a petrol depot. At first it looked hopeless to think of repairing the propeller and going on, and so here we were marooned in a dry and desolate part of Australia, 150 miles from a telegraph and 450 miles from the nearest railway. It was not a pleasing prospect by any means.

Just after we landed we were greatly astonished to see two motorcars coming toward us. It seemed too good to be true, as we thought that we would certainly have to walk the twenty-odd miles to Anthony's Lagoon before we could hope for any assistance.

The cars contained Mr. Sydney Peacock, his son and Sergeant Stretton of the Mounted Police. Mr. Peacock had been sinking a subartesian bore just where we landed and he was now going to remove his camp and travel back into Queensland until after the summer.

Had we arrived an hour later he would have struck his camp and gone and we would have been faced with a long, hot, and dry walk.

We had little food and no water in the Vimy but Mr. Peacock kindly insisted on leaving us all his before he departed, and he arranged to have supplies sent out to us from Anthony's Lagoon. He also left us a sheet of galvanized iron with which Bennett said he could mend the broken propeller.

We were camped there for three and a half days during which time Sergeant Bennett carried out a wonderful, unique piece of skilful workmanship.

When the propeller blade split in the air several splinters of wood had flown off, but Bennett, nothing daunted, shaped new bits out of a piece of packing case to fill the gaps. He next glued the split portions together, then cut the sheet of galvanized iron into strips and bound them round the blade. The strips of iron were fastened onto the blade with screws which we had taken out of the floorboards of the machine. When this was done the whole blade was covered with fabric and painted.

So that there would be little or no vibration the opposite blade of the propeller had to be treated in exactly the same manner.

14,000 Miles Through the Air Ross Smith

'We were camped there for three and a half days ...' Left to right: Ross Smith, Wally Shiers, Keith Smith at Anthony's Lagoon.

The conditions under which we worked were very trying and during the middle of the day it was impossible to do anything except lie in the shade of the wings and pant. The shade temperature underneath the wings was as high as 125° and the heat even melted our goggles and windscreens.

Water was very scarce and none of us washed for the whole three and a half days. The bore which Mr. Peacock had put down contained semi-brackish water and we had to haul it up 150 feet in a small bucket. It was very dirty too as the bore had not been cleaned out since it was made and the water made all of us ill when we drank it.

During the day we wore no clothes except our overalls and boots, but we were really quite happy by ourselves with no one to worry us and ask the same old innumerable questions about the speed of the machine, its weight, where we sat and so forth; it was the first real rest that we had had.

Keith amused me very much one evening. We were having our usual meal of tinned meat and biscuits when he suddenly remarked: 'If we had some ham we would have some ham and eggs, if we had some eggs.'

I believe it is a very old joke, but I had never heard it before and it sounded so very funny away out there and I remember laughing about it for a long while afterward.

During the second night we were camped here a heavy thunderstorm passed over and we managed to collect quite a lot of water as it ran off the wings.

It was a great relief when the propeller was finally fitted on the engine again and so well had Bennett done his work that there was practically no vibration when the engine was running.

From Anthony's Lagoon much of the flight over featureless country would have been drear and monotonous, but it was Australia and that was compensation enough. Moreover, we had the occasional diversion of passing over small outback towns, where many of the inhabitants rushed into the streets and stood looking up, waving and cheering, and wherever we landed there was always a warm welcome awaiting us.

At Charleville in Central Queensland both engines were given a much needed and thorough overhaul and a new propeller was made by the Queensland government at their railway workshop at Ipswich. It was here also that we were joined by my old friend, Captain Frank Hurley of Antarctic fame; he completed the rest of the flight with us in the Vimy taking films and photographs and his cheery optimism and unfailing good humour made us all wish that he had been with us the whole way from England.

The sublimest spectacle of the entire flight from Hounslow to our journey's end was to burst upon us when we arrived over Sydney and its wonderful harbor. Like a mighty fern leaf, ramifying and studded with islets, this glorious waterway unfolded below. The city, massed along the waterfront and extending into the hinterlands, flanked by the Blue Mountains, composed a spectacle of exquisite charm and beauty.

We headed up the coast and, turning through the entrance, entered the port.

Down at 600 feet, we flew above a myriad ferry boats and vessels, from the whistles of which little white jets of steam spurted up, screaming a welcome; then across the roof tops, where crowded waving and cheering humanity, and over the streets below, where little specks paused to look up and join in the greeting. It was a great day – a time that comes once in a lifetime.

Not the least pleasant incident upon our arrival finally in Melbourne was the paying over of the £10 000 prize by Prime Minister Hughes, on behalf of the Commonwealth government. As all participated equally in the perils and labours of the enterprise, the prize was divided into four equal shares.

In Melbourne I formally handed the Vimy over to the Commonwealth government on behalf of Vickers, who generously presented the machine to the Commonwealth as an historic relic of the first aerial flight from London to Australia.

At the request of the authorities, I flew the machine on to Adelaide, my native city, and thus realized to the full my ambition and dream of flying from London to my own home.

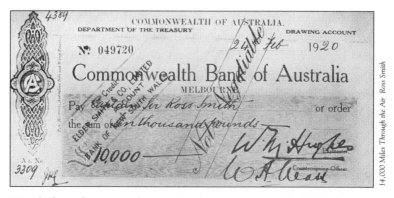

'Not the least pleasant incident ... was the paying over of the £10 000 prize ...'

It would be hard indeed to comprehend the feelings that surged through me as I landed the Vimy on the sod of my native city; the recognition of familiar faces; the greeting of well known voices; the handclasp of innumerable friends; but, greatest of all, the reunion with my parents after five long years.

My brother Keith shares equally any worthiness that the effort might merit, as also do my two master mechanics, Sergeants Bennett and Shiers.

'Labours of the enterprise ...' Working on the Vimy at Sydney.

Our heartfelt thanks are due to the officers and mechanics of the Royal Air Force; to the Dutch authorities for constructing aerodromes and other assistance, and for the cooperation of numerous friends, whose willing and generous help laid the paving stones over which Fortune piloted me.

EDITORS' NOTE: The Smith brothers were knighted immediately by King George V and awarded the Air Force Cross. Wally Shiers and Jim Bennett were awarded a second Air Force Medal each and were commissioned as lieutenants in the Australian Flying Corps.

Ross Smith and Jim Bennett were killed in a crash near the Vickers works at Weybridge, England on Friday 13 April 1922 while preparing for a round-the-world flight in a new aircraft. Ross was just six months short of his thirtieth birthday. Keith Smith was late arriving from London that morning or he, too, would have died in the accident.

Keith Smith became Vickers' representative in Australia and a director of Qantas. He died in 1955, aged sixty-seven.

Wally Shiers married soon after arriving in Australia and later become chief engineer for Airlines of Australia. He died in Adelaide in 1968, aged seventy-nine.

The Vickers Vimy in which they made the journey is preserved in an air-conditioned hangar at Adelaide Airport and can be reached by a walkway with plaques commemorating the stages of the journey. Restored in 1982, The Vimy still carries the British civil registration letters, G-EAOU . . . 'God 'Elp All of Us'.

Across the Pacific

Charles Kingsford Smith

1 THE SOUTHERN CROSS

As his ship is to the sailor and his horse to the rider, so is his plane to the airman. My affection for the *Southern Cross* and admiration for her designer and builders is increased when I reflect on all she has done and all that she has gone through.

The story of the *Southern Cross* really begins on the day (5 August 1927) that I landed in San Francisco with my friends, Charles Ulm and Keith Anderson.

Ulm had similar ideas to mine. He was ambitious; he wanted to do something which would make the world sit up; he had a good business head; in fact, he was a born organiser. Why should we two not capitalise our combined assets?

The Atlantic had been flown several times.

There were other oceans.

Why not fly across the Pacific, the greatest ocean of them all?

This was a feat which should bring us what we wanted, fame, money, status. We wanted also to do something which would not only advance aviation and confound the sceptics, but something that would bring fame to our country.

We had gone over to the United States with a definite idea that we should fly across the Pacific from America to Australia.

Photographer Unknown Southern Cross Trans Pacific Flight

'Why not fly across the Pacific,
the greatest ocean of them all?'
Charles Kingsford Smith.

We landed with but vague notions how such a flight was to be successfully carried out; we had some promises from Australia of financial support and I had had considerable experience of flying in all types of planes in England, America and Australia. But our determination to make the flight was our principal and indeed our only asset when we set foot in the United States. The lack of money has been a common feature in all pioneering efforts. Antarctic explorers such as Shackleton and Amundsen were continually worried by an acute shortage of funds when endeavouring to organize their expeditions; in earlier days, men like Dampier had to beg, borrow or steal ships, men, and money for their intrepid enterprises, and the earliest and greatest of all pioneers, Columbus, spent many a weary month in attempting to interest the rich and powerful in his plans.

We experienced the same disappointments as our great predecessors, and the delays which followed, one after another subsequent to our arrival in the United States, were almost entirely due to our inability to raise the necessary funds wherewith to purchase a suitable machine and its equipment.

We landed in San Francisco from the steamer *Tahiti* on 5 August 1927, but it was not until the morning of 31 May 1928 – nine months later – that we were at last able to set off on the first of our long-distance flights in the *Southern Cross*.

That nine months was a period of anxiety and stress almost more trying than the flight across the Pacific itself.

Shortly after we arrived in the United States, the Dole Race to Hawaii, in which seven lives had been lost, caused an unprecedented slump in aviation in the West. Long flights over the sea became definitely unpopular. The Dole Race had exposed the dangers of heavily overladen machines, of blind flying and of single-engined planes engaged in such ventures, and consequently our arrival at this time could not have been in more unfavourable circumstances.

On the other hand, the lessons of the Dole Race proved very valuable to me. If failures had occurred on the sea route between the mainland and Hawaii, it was quite evident that, on the far longer ocean stretch on which we were to be engaged, the finest and most powerful machine available would be necessary to ensure success and to avoid disaster.

But such a machine, together with its equipment and preparation, and the arrangements for the flight, would cost a great deal more money than the Government of New South Wales had kindly placed at our disposal, even if it were possible to secure the plane. We were perfectly confident, provided we could secure the right machine and the right equipment and organisation, that our proposed flight across the Pacific was not only feasible, but a safe and almost certain venture.

After a prolonged analysis of the best flying performances already recorded in which power and endurance were combined, my inquiries and observation led me to the belief that there was only one design of plane for such a flight – the three-engined Fokker – and only one type of engine – the Wright Whirlwind.

Furthermore, a Fokker plane would enable four of us to make the flight, giving us not only a navigator, but a wireless operator.

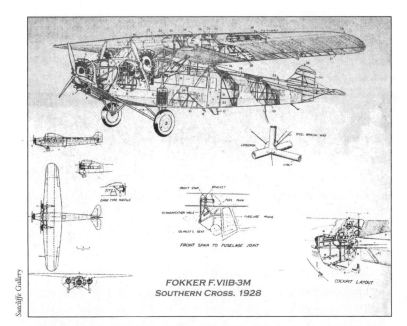

FOKKER F.VIIB-3M
SOUTHERN CROSS. 1928

'There was only one design of plane for such a flight – the three-engined Fokker.' Plans of 'Southern Cross'/'Detroiter'.

Anthony Fokker is one of the world's aeronautic geniuses. While still a youth he designed his first plane, and when the war broke out he offered the Fokker design to the Allies, but the offer, unfortunately in my opinion, was not accepted. He thereupon offered it to the Germans, who eagerly accepted it, much to their advantage, and to the loss of the Allied airmen, during the war.

After the war he set up a large factory in his native city of Amsterdam and began to produce the commercial Fokker plane in large numbers. Finally he was induced to cross over to America, where he became the chief of the Aviation Department of the great General Motors organisation.

Now, by a remarkable coincidence, we were brought into close touch with a Fokker plane. Sir Hubert Wilkins had been flying in the Arctic and had recently given up that season's attempt to fly across the North Pole. He had a Fokker plane which was then superfluous to his requirements, and hearing, while he was in

Seattle, that we were in San Francisco seeking such a plane, he promptly telegraphed to me that he could sell us a Fokker plane without, however, engines or instruments.*

In the course of many long talks with him he not only gave us a great deal of valuable information, but also told us the history of the plane which he was willing to sell to us. It had been built by the Fokker Company during its early days in the United States for use in Alaska, and was known as a Fokker F.7 monoplane.

The machine had crashed on the rough ice, but was later salvaged, and eventually shipped to Seattle and reconditioned by the Boeing factory.

The price Wilkins asked was £3000 and, although we had enough funds to buy the Fokker, we did not have sufficient to purchase the engines and the instruments as well. But again our good fortune held, for at this juncture we met Mr. Sidney Myer, a wealthy Australian businessman.

We asked him to help us in order that we might buy a Fokker plane with three engines in which to fly across the Pacific Ocean.

He was against the proposal, and though he would have liked to have helped us, I felt that he was deterred from doing so lest he should be associated with a venture in which he was convinced we should lose our lives.

When he realised that we were determined to make the attempt, with three engines or with one, Mr Myer generously handed us $1500, and told us it was a gift. Later on he begged us to abandon

*EDITORS' NOTE: The Fokker F.VIIb-3m was derived directly from the single-engined F.VIIa high-wing monoplane. The prototype was built in seven weeks, on the instructions of Anthony Fokker to construct a suitable entrant for him to fly in the 1926 Ford Reliability Tour.

For his 1926 Arctic expedition, fellow countryman George Hubert Wilkins had bought a single-engined F. VIIa and one of the new F. VIIb-3m trimotors, called the *Detroiter* after main sponsor the *Detriot News*. After breaking an arm and suffering a few flying accidents Wilkins postponed his flight and sent *Detroiter* to Seattle for repair. Sir Hubert met with Kingsford Smith and Ulm in San Francisco and the two decided to buy the trimotor without engines and instruments, and to have two additional fuel tanks installed. With those, the Fokker could cross the Pacific. The Wright Whirlwind production schedule was backlogged but the U.S. Secretary of War agreed to deliver three Whirlwinds engines from a government order immediately and accept their later order in return.

'*The machine had crashed on the rough ice, but was later salvaged …*'
The Detroiter – *later to become the* Southern Cross.

'*It had been built by the Fokker Company during its early days in the United States for use in Alaska.*'

Across the Pacific ~ 179

the project altogether, at the same time reiterating that the money which he had given us was ours to do as we liked with.

I thanked him for his great generosity and kindness to us, but told him that we were fully determined to make the flight, that nothing would induce us to abandon our plans, and that with the help of the money he had given us we had decided to buy Wilkins' plane.

But the further funds which we needed to buy the engines had not arrived from Australia. In this dilemma Wilkins came to the rescue by allowing us to pay only half the purchase price for the plane, which enabled us to place the order for the three engines.

We now had the plane, and the engines were on order.

Despite the difficulties and delays that had occurred I began to feel that things were going very well, but now we were to receive another rude shock. We found that the factory that made the Wright Whirlwind engines was already eighty or ninety engines behind with its orders, and that months might, and probably would, elapse before our turn came.

In our trouble we went to Mr. Locke T. Harper, the West Coast representative of the Vacuum Oil Company, who had proved to be a very good friend to us. Through Lieutenant B. Wyatt, USN, Mr. Harper was able to secure us an introduction to Rear Admiral Peables, commanding the Western Naval district.

At first Wyatt and the admiral were against listening to our story at all. But when we explained that we proposed to fly in a three-motored Fokker and that we would carry a crew of four, including two pilots, a navigator and a wireless operator, their attitude changed at once, and from thence onward they afforded us every assistance.

Once again the outlook grew brighter, and we engaged Phil C. Salzman, an experienced engineer, and George A. Hedinger, a very capable mechanic, to supervise the delivery and installation of the engines which had been promised us.

Meanwhile Keith Anderson had left for the Hawaiian Islands to inspect Wheeler Field and Barking Sands, both 'taking off' places for the second section of the flight from Hawaii to Fiji. It was most important that we should choose the better of the two, as the *Southern Cross* would be loaded down to capacity and I wanted first-hand information about the takeoff.

We wanted the most powerful wireless equipment that could be carried with the least possible weight, and in our search for the right gear we were making good progress. Everything, in short, seemed to be in train when another blow befell us.

From our native land appeals now came from individuals, from the press, and finally from the government urging us to abandon this foolhardy venture. There was deep concern for our safety on such a flight as we proposed to make.

Our plans were now too far advanced to enable us to abandon the flight, even had we been willing to do so.

We had ordered numerous navigating and pilotage instruments; I had secured the services of Lieutenant G. R. Pond, a very experienced Fokker pilot, to co-operate with me in the first tests of the machine; Anderson had now returned with his report that Wheeler Field was the place at which to land and Barking Sands the best from which to 'take off,' and, furthermore, as Wilkins, who was now making ready for his second Polar flight, needed money to complete payments on his own plane, I felt that we could not possibly fail him.

We were thus deeply indebted financially, while our organisation for the flight was far advanced. There seemed to be no way out of the impasse. We had to secure money, and at once.

2 ENDURANCE

Casting our minds for some way of raising funds, we hit upon the idea of endeavouring to break the world's record for sustained flight, which then stood at 52 hours 22 minutes. Pond and I would make an attempt to beat the world's record endurance flight, which meant that we had to remain in the air without refuelling for the maximum possible time.

The plane was flown from San Francisco to Santa Monica, near Los Angeles, where it was prepared for the stern test before us.

Such a venture necessitated loading up the *Southern Cross* with petrol to the limit – and beyond it.

She was so overladen that it was a desperate effort to leave the ground.

It was on the morning of 17 January 1928, that Pond and I took our seats in the cockpit of the *Southern Cross* to make our attempt on the world's non-refuelling endurance record. The task which we were about to essay was to remain in the air for a longer period than 52 hours 22 minutes, which record had been set up by two German airmen, Risticz and Edzard, in a Junkers J3 monoplane, flying continuously over a 60 mile circuit at Leipzig in the previous August.

It was a fine, calm morning though rather cold as the *Southern Cross* waited, with her huge tanks filled, on the runway at Mills' Field, San Francisco. We had stripped her of every possible portion of equipment which would add to her weight; we had filled her tanks with petrol to the total of 1522 gallons, so that she weighed over seven instead of the normal five tons.

We had previously had her fitted with new stub axles and specially built wheels to support the enormous load; we had even divested her of her brakes to save weight; and we had shed everything in order to make her as light as possible, our only concern being to load her with fuel to her maximum capacity.

There is, of course, a limit to which a plane can be 'composite loaded,' and flown. Our wing loading in pounds per square foot was a total load of 49.5 – the heaviest composite load ever lifted by any plane.

The *Southern Cross* groaned under the burden. Her gross weight was 15,807 pounds – over seven tons – and we faced the problem of adequate control of the machine, for we knew it was possible to 'take off' with a plane so heavily loaded, she will not fly.

Due to the cushioning effect of the air against the ground by the loaded wing surface, a heavily loaded plane will not gain altitude much greater than the span of her wings. In this condition a plane is in a highly dangerous state as the slightest 'slip' would take away this cushioning effect and inevitably end in a crash.

We had strengthened the whole tail end of the body, fitted extra vertical members at points of maximum stress in the fuselage, installed special flexible petrol pipe to withstand the vibration, built in stronger axles to take the great weight, and our wheels and tyres were especially strong. But it must be remembered that in those days the *Southern Cross* was one of the largest planes in existence, and we were in the pioneering days of heavy load flying.

An endurance flight of the kind we were about to make had three advantages from my point of view. In the first place, there was the chance that we might break the existing record and thereby win a monetary prize, which we urgently needed.

In the second place, we were giving the plane the very tests which were necessary before we could hope to make the Pacific flight, and we were gathering valuable knowledge of her exact capacity, power and endurance, though we needed range in miles rather than range in hours.

Finally, an endurance test, with its appalling monotony during long hours in the air, was a good test for me personally, and gave me useful preparation for the long hours ahead when we should embark on our long distance flights.

We had already made four attempts, but three of them had proved abortive, as we had been unable to remain in the air for any appreciable time. On the fourth attempt we had been more successful, remaining in the air for 49 hours 27 minutes, but this was still far short of the record, and we realised that we should have to make a supreme effort on this fifth and last occasion.

In the course of these preliminary flights we had discovered many matters which required adjustment, notably what is termed 'tail flutter'. Tail flutter is a vibration set up in the rear control surfaces of a machine heavily loaded and flying too slowly; or conversely of a machine flying lightly loaded and too fast.

Mills' Field, where the takeoff was to be made, had a runway of 4900 feet. The field was an extensive open ground which had been reclaimed from the sea by a levee built round the field. This levee was about 10 feet high, and in front of it was a ditch about 20 feet wide and 5 feet deep.

A small crowd had gathered to watch our takeoff, including many aviation experts and enthusiasts who were aware of the grave difficulties and risks confronting us in taking off.

When all was ready, the propellers were swung and there was a terrific roar which gradually increased as we warmed up the engines to get the oil sufficiently hot, thereby lessening the friction and increasing the revolutions.

At last the chocks under the wheels were removed, the bystanders stood back, we opened the three throttles to their utmost, and imperceptibly the *Southern Cross* began to move forward. We had 4900 feet of runway ahead of us – and no more. Beyond the runway was the levee which we had to clear. With the engines roaring full out, the plane dragged herself along at no more than a walking pace.

It seemed an interminable time before she began to gather momentum, but gradually the pace increased as the powerful engines gathered revs.

At the 2000 feet mark our tail began to leave the ground and soon after we reached a stage at which our increasing speed was sufficient to just lift her off the ground. We were, in fact, now moving at almost the minimum speed necessary to take off – 90 miles an hour.

I glanced ahead. The levee, which seemed to tower in front of us, was advancing at a terrific rate. Pond was at the controls. I glanced at him. His jaw was set – his gaze fixed on the levee.

My hand was on the dump valve, fitted to the main petrol tank, for in a last frantic effort to clear the levee I was to dump the petrol at the last moment. At 3000 feet along the runway we had to make a decision whether we would clear the bank or not.

This was an appalling responsibility. If we decided that we could not clear it, we had to try and bring up the machine in the short run left to us. She was then tearing along at over 90 mph – and we had jettisoned our brakes.

On the other hand, if we decided that we might just clear it, there was only one thing to do – to leave the throttles wide open and charge on at utmost speed.

We charged on. Some instinct peculiar to airmen told us that the old bus would make it.

The gallant plane was now 'all out'. When we were still about 300 yards off, the wheels left the ground for a few inches. Then they settled again . . . and we were on the last hundred yards!

We deliberately pushed forward the controls. The effect was to drive the machine downwards. At that speed the contact with the ground developed into a bump.

We had bounced the now flying machine over the levee.

We had cleared the levee, but the overladen machine was still staggering within a few inches of the water that lay beyond it. We flew on for a further mile or so, lying dangerously low until we found that it was possible gradually to lift the machine to some degree of altitude.

We did not wish to expend petrol in climbing; we desired urgently to close down the throttles as soon as possible to save fuel, and so gradually, as the petrol load decreased, we throttled slightly back at a height of about 500 feet, always endeavouring to maintain a nice balance between the maximum speed for safety and the minimum for consumption. This meant holding the plane at stalling point all the time – a highly risky proceeding with an overloaded machine.

Nevertheless, we had to save fuel in every possible way.

That fifty hours which I spent in the air with Pond circling round and round San Francisco Bay will always remain a nightmare to me.

It was bitterly cold; we could communicate only with pencilled notes to each other; we were cramped in the cockpit, since the passage away to the rear compartment was filled with petrol tanks; we couldn't smoke; we couldn't sleep; we had to maintain our wits at their sharpest, for at our low flying speed we were always near to stalling.

The weary day passed; night fell; the winter mists of San Francisco Bay gathered, forcing us to climb the still overloaded machine to 1,000 feet for greater safety; our eyes were fixed on the petrol gauges; occasionally we had a sandwich or a hot drink out of our thermos flask, and gradually, as our decreasing load would permit, we lessened the engine revolutions to save fuel.

We faced the second day, tired but hopeful.

The petrol gauges still held out some promise that we might be enabled to remain in the air longer than our German rivals.

Above our heads was the sealed barograph fitted by the representatives of the *Fédération Aéronautique Internationale*. It contained a revolving cylinder with an aneroid barometer attached, and recorded our altitude as well as the time in the air.

Towards the end of the second day we began to realise with dismay that our fuel consumption was greater than we had estimated. Our petrol was highly volatile, and the cold air necessitated more being fed into the carburettors. But we still held on, determined to see our fuel exhausted before we would land.

Round we circled, at low speed, round and round a 50 mile circuit over San Francisco Bay. I think I know every smallest feature of that bay – it is indelibly printed on my mind.

The second night fell, one of the worst nights I have ever experienced.

To add to our physical discomfort was the feeling that we were failing. We were weary and haggard, it was bitterly cold and I craved a warm bed and sleep.

At dawn we realised that the game was up, and at 7.30 am I wirelessed to the ground: *Southern Cross* will be compelled to land at 9.30 am, running out of fuel. She cannot lift enough fuel for more than 50 hours. It is just livable up here. That's all.'

At 9.30 am we decided, with mutual shrugs of disappointment, that we had failed, and that the time had come to descend.

We landed at 10.13 am on 19 January having been 50 hours and 4 minutes in the air, according to the official timekeeper. We were so thoroughly tired and chilled that we could hardly speak or stand, and we were stone deaf.

We had failed to beat the record, but the *Southern Cross* had not failed us. She had lifted a weight of fuel equivalent to that of 68 people.

We had failed to break the record, and we had failed to win the money prize that was so urgently needed.

Keith Anderson, who had formed one of the original party, and had stayed loyally with us through all these trials and troubles, explained that as there seemed now to be no prospect of the Pacific flight being made and that as we had come to the end of our funds he felt obliged to yield to the wishes of his relatives and friends to return to Australia.

It seemed to me the wisest thing to do – the only thing to do, though Ulm and I were sorry to lose him.

The sun of our fortunes seemed to be setting when a little later we received an intimation that the New South Wales government desired us to sell the plane and return to Australia.

It really seemed that there was nothing more to be done. We had now been six months in the United States and were no nearer achieving our ambition than when we arrived. Our creditors were pressing us and it was evident that we could expect no further assistance from our government. We were under orders to sell the *Southern Cross* (if we could) and to return to Australia.

We were absolutely penniless, and moreover were heavily in debt. We were so poor that we had not even loose cash in our pockets to purchase cigarettes or a meal. We were unable to pay our hotel bill and were driven to all sorts of subterfuges to stave off those to whom we owed money.

We had, in fact, reached rock bottom.

It was necessary to go to Los Angeles, where we hoped to be able to sell the *Southern Cross* to the Union Oil Company of California. But we had no money to pay our train fare. However, we managed to obtain some petrol and oil, and for want of any other means of reaching Los Angeles we flew there in the plane.

We were so desperate that we offered to do anything. We were prepared to fly to Australia or anywhere else as employees of the company, but though the company's officials were sympathetic the negotiations broke down. It was the darkest hour, for we had now lost hope and it seemed that all our labours had been in vain.

But suddenly the whole situation changed as if by magic.

3 Captain Hancock

We were standing gloomily at the Rogers Airport near Los Angeles one day early in March when the president of the Californian Bank of Los Angeles (Mr. Andrew Chaffey) introduced us to Captain G. Allan Hancock.

We found that Captain Hancock was much interested in navigation, that he was himself a master mariner, that he was very interested in the navigation of our proposed flight across the Pacific, and finally that he was wealthy.

Much to our delight, he very kindly invited Ulm and me to accompany him on a cruise in his steam yacht *Oaxaca*. He plied us with questions, and I really think he had invited us on that cruise in order 'to size us up'.

Anyhow, two days before we landed on the return from that wonderful cruise, he suddenly asked us how much money we needed to solve our dilemma.

We told him – $3200.

There was silence for a moment. Then he spoke: 'I'll buy the machine from you, boys,' he said. 'I'll see my solicitors and decide the best way to do it.'

We were overjoyed! The great flight was at once brought closer to us. It was no longer an impossible dream, and all our labours had not been in vain. Captain Hancock was as good as his word. A few days later Captain Hancock became the owner of the *Southern Cross*, told us that we might fly her to Australia, and advanced us funds to carry out our plans.

There was still a great deal to be done before we should be ready for the flight. A new fabric cover for the fuselage was needed, and the wing required repairs and reconditioning. Keith Anderson had returned to Australia, and as we wanted him to make the flight with us, we cabled him to return. So that he might have time we asked Captain Hancock if we might delay the start of the flight until the end of May, to which he agreed; but Anderson, to my regret, was unable to join the new venture.

It was Keith Anderson, by the way, who suggested the name *Southern Cross*.

And now ensued six busy weeks of preparation unhampered by any further money troubles.

For safety purposes, I planned an average speed on the flight of only 90 miles, at 1600 rpm, with a fuel consumption of 32 gallons per hour. As our total supply was 1298 gallons, this gave us a range of 40½ hours, which, at 90 miles an hour (assuming still air), was equal to 3645 miles.

Our longest 'hop', from Kauai, in the Hawaiian Islands, to Suva, would be 3128 miles, giving us a margin of over 500 miles.

Many people have wondered why we chose a land plane to fly across an ocean. The answer is that at the time of our flight there was no three or four engined amphibian or flying boat available, and in any case the cost of such an amphibian would have been far beyond our capacity.

As it was, the *Southern Cross* would have probably saved our lives, even if we had been forced down on to the sea. The whole of the giant wing was entirely of wood, and in itself could have kept the craft afloat.

We also fitted a special dump valve to the main tank (807 gallons), which would have enabled us to empty the tank in about 50 seconds. This dump valve could be resealed, thus giving extra buoyancy. With steel and wood saws we could have cut off the outboard motors, and the whole of the fuselage, thus converting the wing into a large raft, unhampered by any heavy gear. In the wing we carried emergency rations, and we also had a special small distilling plant, enabling us to condense drinking water.

The enormous advantage of having three engines lay in the fact that at most stages of the flight we could have reached land with two engines running. Even with only one engine in operation we could have stayed in the air for sufficient time to allow SOS calls for assistance to be transmitted.

We were thus well provided against undue risks. We had an ample reserve of fuel; we had three engines; we had the capacity to remain afloat for an indefinite period if forced down on to the sea; we had a radio transmitting plant wherewith to call for assistance; we had made arrangements to keep our navigating instruments and nautical tables with us.

If shipwrecked, we had emergency rations, and a small distilling plant to save us from hunger and thirst; and, in the *Southern Cross* herself and her engines, we had a plane which I was confident would see us through.

But a great deal would depend on the man who would navigate us on this long flight, and the wireless operator on whose skill and efficiency our lives might depend.

There is a great deal of difference between the leisurely navigation of a ship from a comfortable bridge and navigation from a small cabin of an aeroplane. The mariner is limited to visibility of a few miles, the airman in clear weather can see an island up to 100 miles away.

In addition to navigating by dead reckoning based on our known speed and our compass course corrected for wind drift, we relied on astronomical navigation and navigation aided by wireless beacons.

Wireless navigation, which was of great value to us on the first stage of the flight, was in those days based on a wireless beam sent out from the radio station at Crissy Field, the direction of the beam being in a direct line to Honolulu. Similarly from Honolulu another beam was transmitted in a north-easterly direction toward San Francisco. On the first stage of the flight, we hoped to keep on the line of the Crissy Field beam until it waned, when we hoped to pick up the Honolulu beam.

With Captain Hancock behind us, things now proceeded very smoothly. The plane was overhauled and put into first-class condition at the Douglas Factory at Santa Monica. To supervise the installation and trials of the three Wright Whirlwind engines we were fortunate in securing the services of Mr. C. C. Maidment, who had been Lindbergh's engineer, and I do not think any greater testimony is required.

Our compasses were tested by Captain J. T. McMillan, who was chief of the hydrographic office in San Francisco, and an acknowledged authority on navigation.

We asked him if he could secure us the services of an expert navigator, and he strongly recommended Captain Harry Lyon to us. We were at once taken with Lyon, whose wide experience as a navigator both in the navy and merchant service, and adventurous nature and clear thinking combined to give him the very qualities for the job.

Lyon, in turn, introduced to us James Warner, who was an experienced radioman, and had been shipmates with Lyon. We could not have had a more efficient man than Warner, and his excellent work on the flight across the Pacific amply justified the faith we had in him.

As for Lyon, in addition to navigating by dead reckoning based on our known speed and compass course, he relied on both astronomical navigation and Warner's radio beam readings.

In steering a course we relied on an earth inductor compass, the generator of which was mounted in the tail, having two other compasses in addition.

Those experts who had previously criticised our projected flight were now becoming far more tolerant than when we had first announced our plans. It became known that we were perfecting our equipment and organisation to a point which ruled out any question of a haphazard dash without adequate preparation.

Furthermore, we were fortunate enough to possess the co-operation and assistance of high authorities, including senior officers in the army and navy, the weather bureau and the signal corps.

The weather bureau co-operated by giving us their weather forecasts and conditions, and the army radio station at Crissy Field promised to aid our navigation by sending out a continuous wireless beam in the course to Honolulu.

Nevertheless, in spite of all these arrangements, preparations and precautions, a number of people still prophesied disaster, and shook their heads dolefully at the prospects before us.

The exact date of our departure depended entirely on the first reasonably good weather forecast combined with a full moon. We only waited now for weather.

The evening before we took off we received a satisfactory weather report from the meteorological officers. The moon was full, we were all ready to start. There was nothing further to delay us.

I retired to bed that night ready for the departure in the morning, filled with confidence.

4 WESTWARD HO!

I have a vivid recollection of the morning of 31 May 1928, when with a roar of the engines, we took off from Oakland airport.

The morning was misty, but the weather forecast was good. As we headed out over the Golden Gate I experienced a sensation of relaxation and relief from worries and anxieties of the past nine months, along with a tremendous elation at the prospect before me.

To me, personally, all our troubles were over. What lay in front was a glorious adventure – and a glorious achievement.

It is true that others had pioneered the path before us as far as Hawaii, but after that we were going into the unknown. Balbao had been the first white man to set eyes on the Pacific; Magellan had been the first to furrow its water with his keel; Bligh had navigated its unknown waters for 3000 miles in an open boat. I felt that we were following in the footsteps of these great predecessors, and that we could claim kinship with them. They had traversed virgin waters; we were about to traverse virgin air.

Photographer Unknown Southern Cross Trans Pacific Flight

'... we were about to traverse virgin air.' Lyon, Smithy, Ulm and Warner.

On my finger I wore a silver ring. Just as we were leaving the ground I had been approached by Mrs. Eichwaldt, the mother of Lieutenant Albert Eichwaldt, who had perished with W. P. Erwin while searching for Miss Doran after the Dole Race disasters. She bade me God speed, and then asked me to wear the ring which her son had made from a franc piece while serving in the war. The incident touched me deeply and I gladly assented to her wish.

And now below lay the Golden Gate shimmering in the haze and our bows were pointed Westward ho!

The outlook was most propitious. Not a single 'low' or depression was on the weather chart. Between Ulm and me fluttered a small Australian flag. As we roared out over the Farallones the wind caught it and tore it to shreds, but I left it there with its tattered remnants, feeling that anyhow we should not 'strike our flag'.

Now that we were well away I had time to look around and size up our situation. The engines were revolving perfectly; their roar prevented any conversation, so that we were forced to rely on pencilled notes, and though I was dying for a cigarette I realised that there would be no cigarettes for any of us until we made Wheeler Field.

Beside me in the cockpit sat Ulm, and in the aftercabin, though I could not see them, were Warner and Lyon, the former busily engaged in receiving and transmitting radio messages, and listening for the buzz of the wireless beam, while Lyon was continually checking our course, speed and drift.

My chief concern was with the engines and with the weather ahead of us.

The roar of those three great Whirlwinds, which in trial flights had grated heavily on my eardrums, became now a harmonious overture, to which I listened hour after hour with an ear attuned to catch the slightest hesitancy in their beat.

On the engines everything depended, and God knows they had a tremendous call upon them for I demanded that they should maintain an average of 1600 revolutions per minute for three prolonged periods of 27½ hours, 34½ hours and 20 hours.

My next concern was with the weather ahead particularly the probability of running into the cloud we feared and hoped to avoid. We wished to fly somewhere less than 2000 feet to avoid clouds, as it was the climbing above the clouds that ate up our petrol.

Right through the flight it was our aim to fly as low as was consistent with safety.

Our petrol consumption was, in fact, my chief source of anxiety. Though I was convinced in my heart of hearts that we had ample reserves to give us a wide margin, doubts continually assailed me.

Perhaps it was the knowledge of the petrol in the tank near me that drew my mind again and again to this matter as the *Southern Cross* roared on her way above the sea spread out below us. Perhaps the motors were eating up more petrol than I thought, and after the first few hours, when I had to climb to nearly 3000 feet to avoid ranges of cloud, the fear that more climbing might be in front of us worried me.

Our speed was between 70 and 80 knots, and at noon, when the navigator put on the clock 15 minutes, we were going strong and had covered 340 miles of the 2000 which lay before us.

It began to be monotonous. In the cockpit, where Ulm and I sat, there was just room to stretch for a doze, but our sleep was not restful.

As the day drew on, the monotony increased but we were enlivened from time to time by cheery little messages from Lyon, who maintained a regular delivery of notes which told us where we were, and at other times asked us most unexpected questions.

The flying conditions were perfect, but the monotony of the blue sea below us, the blue vault above us, and the overpowering roar of the engines began to oppress us. I yearned to get out and stretch my limbs and urgently wanted a cigarette. But that was taboo.

One of the remarkable things about this flight was the almost entire absence of any shipping. Quite a fleet of steamers was supposed to be on the course between Frisco and Honolulu, but we sighted only two, and both of these at night.

By six o'clock that evening we had been flying for nine hours at an average speed of 78 miles an hour. We had covered 700 miles and still had 1390 to go. Away on the starboard bow the sun was setting in a great ball of fire and I witnessed such a spectacular and glorious sunset as I had seldom seen before.

We climbed to 4000 feet as darkness descended. Everything was going well, except for the physical discomfort and stiffness due to our cramped quarters and the mental strain imposed by the necessity of being continually on the alert and keeping all my wits sharpened.

The moon was astern of us, and we flew along over the silver path which she cast on the sea below. Overhead, in the clear night air, the stars looked down on us as we roared on.

At ten o'clock Lyon cast overboard the calcium flares which he used with the drift meter to check our drift. They struck the water and burst into a white blaze, and we watched them for about twenty minutes. They indicated a very slight southerly drift, and showed we were keeping our course well.

Just before midnight we ran into some heavy clouds at 4000 feet and then rain. It was the first time we had struck rain, and for some minutes I was flying blind, climbing to 4800 feet, when fortunately we cleared it and all was serene again.

At midnight we were at 5400 feet; our speed was 67 knots; we calculated that we had 570 gallons in the tanks; everything was proceeding 'according to plan'.

Just before 2 am we caught sight of some pinpoints of light below us on the port side and made out the dark hull of a steamer. It was the first sign of human activity we had seen since leaving land, and I felt a friendly feeling towards this only other occupant of the vast and dark space beneath us.

While Ulm took the controls and headed the *Southern Cross* towards her, I called her up with our searchlight, fitted with a Morse key for signalling, and flashed 'OKSC' for 'OK *Southern Cross*'.

She signalled her name, *Maliko*, one of the Matson Line's ships, and from her Warner received a radio bearing which gave us a fix on our position.

All the time at regular intervals Warner was sending various radio messages which were heard, not only over the United States, but also in Honolulu.

In addition to these brief official messages, we occasionally sent out more unconventional messages to various friends of the crew, nearly all of which were duly received and transmitted to the addressees.

Soon after we had passed the *Maliko*, Warner was in touch with the *Manoa*. We were then at 4600 feet and going well at 65 knots, and a little later I sighted her lights far away below us. Ulm once again flew the *Southern Cross* towards her while I signalled with the seachlight.

These were the only two ships we met in the whole course of the flight across the Pacific. They both belonged to the same line and we sighted them both within an hour of each other. By a quarter to three the *Manoa*'s lights had disappeared astern and we were alone on the trackless void once more.

Meantime the outboard wing tanks containing 192 gallons were empty and we had six hours yet to go before reaching Wheeler Field.

We longed for the dawn. The night was chill and though my wicker chair was roomy and comfortable, allowing me to stretch out my legs, while Ulm relieved me at the controls, the loud deafening roar of the engines allowed only fitful and uneasy sleep.

A lightening of the eastern horizon heralded the dawn a few minutes before six. It was very chilly; we were flying at over 6000 feet at this time to keep above the clouds and the ocean was concealed from sight. All through the night, as our load had been decreasing, we had been steadily increasing our altitude to get above the clouds and also to seek a slight following wind to help us on our way.

All through the night, too, the engines had roared on with regular and faith inspiring monotony. Our worries over the petrol supply were now almost, if not entirely, gone. We were able to check the supply and found we had sufficient left.

Lyon, having got his position, passed through a note to say he calculated we were 330 miles from the nearest land.

The new day cheered us up and a growing sense of achievement filled us. I was able now to bring the plane down by easy stages from 7500 feet to 1700 feet, where we were below the curtain of cloud.

We now began to look out for the land and frequently thought we had sighted one or more of the many islands which form the group.

First Ulm thought he saw land on the port bow and we shook hands, only to find it was cloud.

About ten o'clock I could have sworn that the island of Molokai was on our port bow, but it was not an island – only another cloud.

These deceptive appearances led to some confusion among those at Honolulu who were anxiously awaiting news of us since we 'told the world' on the wireless that we had sighted land, as we thought, and then we had made a mistake. The truth is, of course, that we were not so certain of our position approaching the Hawaiian Islands, but there was no question of our being 'lost' or losing our way. We were merely 'sighting islands' before they actually came into our view.

Suddenly – it was 10.52 am – the real terra firma did appear, far away on the port bow.

As we approached, it did not dissolve like the other apparitions, but stayed put. It was the lofty peak of Mauna Kea, snowcapped, 12 000 feet high.

Then, almost immediately afterwards, other landmarks swam into our ken. There was Maui on the port side; there was Molokai on the port bow, and soon the bold promontory of Diamond Head guided us in towards Wheeler Field.

We passed over Honolulu, gleaming white in the sunlight below us, and headed on the last lap to Wheeler Field, 22 miles away. A number of planes appeared in the air escorting us to the landing ground, and at 12.17 pm, as the *Southern Cross* glided down, I throttled back the engine preparatory to landing. I taxied the machine to the position indicated by one of the US Army Air Force men and switched off all three engines.

The sudden cessation of the roar of the engines left me feeling blank and wondering what had happened. I realised that the roar of

'So far, so good …' Southern Cross *at Honolulu.*

the engines was still going in my head, and as I stepped out of the machine I caught sight of a sea of faces advancing on me from every direction. The next moment we were swallowed up by the crowd.

So far, so good, but this was only the first of three stages, and the second and most arduous lay ahead – the longest ocean flight ever attempted.

5 To Fiji

I should here explain that probably the greatest problem of long distance flying is the question of landing and taking off grounds.

Long-distance flying implies a very heavily laden machine, which in turn necessitates a first class and lengthy runway, with ample scope for the machine to gather speed before she takes the air. In the course of the many flights in the *Southern Cross* I sometimes found myself in difficulties in making a landing, and still greater difficulties in taking off.

Wheeler Field was good for landing, but Barking Sands – so called because of the peculiar noise made by the sand – was better for our takeoff.

We had already arranged for a supply of petrol to be there, and on the afternoon following our landing I climbed into the *Southern Cross* once more to take her on the short flight of 90 miles to the beach of Kauai Island. I landed here without difficulty at six o'clock.

An inspection of the beach reassured me, for it was in much better condition than I had expected. A gang of men had cleared a runway of 4500 feet since, for our load of 1300 gallons of petrol, I judged that we should not be clear of the ground until the plane had travelled at least 3500 feet.

The weather reports were satisfactory, and we were anxious to push on, despite the doleful prediction of a number of people that the next stage would prove our undoing.

We rose at 3 am, and drove to the beach. It was a warm and rather muggy morning; the air was still, the sea calm, and the moon was bright as we climbed into the cockpit to warm up the motors.

At 5.20 am Ulm and I gave the signal for the start. The *Southern Cross* dashed along the sands in beautiful style, and we were off.

But the next moment my confidence was rudely disturbed. We had only climbed about 300 feet when we struck a succession of bumps which made the plane bounce and jerk in a most alarming manner in our heavily laden condition.

For a few moments it needed the greatest care to ease the jolts, but they soon passed, and we settled down on our course on the long, long trail.

Everything now depended on the accuracy of our navigation, for we were making 'a long shot at a dot on the map', and that dot was over 3000 miles away.

Fortunately, from Wheeler Field they were still sending out a radio beam to guide us on the way, and we had to carry this helpful buzz for about 700 miles on the stage. The weather was magnificent, the sea was calm; the sun was shining, and I was able to fly low at about 600 feet, thus conserving our petrol.

Altogether we felt in high spirits at this successful beginning, but Ulm suddenly nudged me and pointed to the wing tank.

I looked and saw a slight trickle of liquid oozing out and running along the steel of the lower part of the wing. Steadily it ran along the wing and dropped into the cockpit. If this were a petrol leak, the possibilities were dreadful to contemplate. I handed over the controls to Ulm and with my heart in my mouth placed a finger on the drop of liquid, and tasted it.

Glory be! It wasn't petrol – only water formed from the condensation of the air around the cold petrol pipe.

The incident passed, but the memory of it remained with us for some time.

Now we were buzzing along at 500 feet and making 80 knots. I was worried by the clouds ahead, which looked like rain, and I couldn't spare petrol to climb above it, nor did I like the thought of flying low in our overladen state.

While my thoughts were busy with these possibilities, Warner passed through a note. He had lost the buzz of the radio beam from Wheeler Field, and we were only three hours out!

But worse was to follow, for shortly after 10 am Warner passed through another note to say that the wireless was completely out of action.

I didn't like it at all, for we were now cut off from the world entirely, but somehow I felt that Warner would get the radio going again, and sure enough he did.

About three hours later he passed through another note: 'Both transmitters working OK.'

Meantime the breeze was freshening, and was helping us along, so that I estimated our ground speed must be at least 90 knots, which was very gratifying. But the weather was deteriorating, and soon we were bucking into rainstorms, trying to dodge them, flying round them and up and through them.

This was very trying, for at times we were flying 'blind', and the climbing was taking a toll of our petrol.

In blind flying you can see through the windshield but not beyond it, because there your visibility ends. Your sight, therefore, is of little or no value. You are blindfolded.

At noon Lyon reported that we had made good 630 nautical miles. Our average speed over the ground was still maintained at 90 knots, and despite the rainstorms we were getting along well. We were cheered, too, a little later, by Warner's note that the wireless was functioning again.

The weather was hot and muggy, and there were thunderstorms all round us, but we were making excellent progress and we had the thrill of being the first to fly into this region.

> We were the first
> That ever burst
> Into that unknown sea.

Then we had another fright. About half-past three that afternoon the starboard motor suddenly coughed.

It was the first time since we had left Oakland that the monotonous roar of the engines had been interrupted by even so slight a sound. A tremendous cough was followed by a splutter and kick.

Then it died away and the engines roared on.

Again we heard it. What could it be? Even Lyon and Warner had noticed it, and passed a note through to ask what was wrong.

We were nearly a thousand miles from the nearest land; we were in mid-ocean – an ocean which, viewed from above, looked grim and menacing.

The cough and splutter continued for about eight minutes. Then it ceased. To this day I have never been certain in my own mind what caused the temporary irregularity, but it was probably a minute speck of dirt or some foreign substance which had passed through the petrol filter and caused a passing disturbance.

Anyhow it was the first and last time on that flight that the rhythmic chorus of the three motors was interrupted.

At 5.30 pm we had been flying for 12 hours, and had covered 1080 nautical miles, approximately one-third of the distance.

The daylight began to wane and I started to climb for the night flying. There were several advantages in this. First, it was safer to be at a good altitude in the hours of darkness and, secondly, there was a possibility of being able to keep above the clouds which were thickening and increasing all round us. Thirdly, by climbing, we prolonged the day, for the higher we went the longer we kept the rays of the sinking sun in view.

But this climbing was eating into our petrol and was getting us nowhere. We wanted horizontal flight – not vertical. Yet by 6.20 we had ascended to 3000 feet. And then the clouds burst, the heavens opened, and the rain swept down on us.

It poured in torrents, and the rain forced its way through the windshield, so that we were sodden from the knees down. We passed 5000 feet, but still those great, coal black clouds encompassed us.

Round and round we went in a spiral climb, seeking to escape from them, and all the time I felt that we were burning up our precious fuel and getting no nearer to Suva.

At length, at a height of 8000 feet, we finally emerged from the murk and gloom.

Above us were the stars, and suddenly I became aware of the Southern Cross glittering on the port bow and, shortly before midnight, Lyon passed a note: 'Just crossed the Equator'. We were in our own hemisphere again.

Here was no languorous tropic sea over which we were flying, but a series of wicked thunderstorms. It was a real 'wet belt,' and it seemed as if we should never get clear of it. Rain and cloud, cloud and rain, was the tale all through the night, with visibility at times nil.

At midnight we expected to sight one or more of the Phoenix Islands about which we had received a mass of information at Honolulu.

The moon was shining, lighting up the face of the waters, and for over an hour we scanned the surface of the sea, looking for the islands. And yet we never saw a sign of any of them.

Our course had been set to pass over the group and it was evident that we were off the track. Accordingly the navigator set what he believed to be a true course direct to Suva.

The fact that we made the flight from Honolulu to Suva without sighting any landmark is further proof of Lyon's skill as a navigator. Had he been able to check our position by sighting the Phoenix Group his task would have been made much easier; but as it was, he was forced to rely on his own calculations, which our arrival at Suva proved to be abundantly justified.

Now ensued another of those long dawn watches, from midnight to daybreak, which we found the most trying of the whole 24 hours.

I was beginning to feel ragged and weary; my clothes were wet from the rain, but fortunately it was fairly warm and we had no need of our furlined overalls.

The dawn came with heavy black cumulus and nimbus clouds around and ahead of us; thunder and lightning in every direction, torrents of rain and wild air currents which bumped the plane about to such an extent that we were pitched all over the place.

We had now been 24 hours in the air, and the worst appeared to be still ahead of us, where a heavy black storm with lightning loomed up 12 000 feet high. There was only one thing to do – glide down under it or get round it somehow, since it was quite impossible for us to try to climb to that height and get above it.

I brought the plane right down to 400 feet, and even lower, until Warner was obliged to reel in the radio aerial. But it was no better down there, so off we went up again, all the time worrying about the way in which we were eating up our petrol.

Another disadvantage of this climbing and twisting and turning to evade the storms was that it confused the navigator, who had the greatest difficulty in maintaining his dead reckoning in such circumstances.

No wonder that Lyon's dead reckoning position at six o'clock that morning was plotted more in hope than in faith that it was correct. He placed us 690 nautical miles from Suva, which was about seven hours' flying.

Seven hours later our logbook records: 'Suva in sight ahead'.

At six o'clock, however, we had been flying for hours intermittently blind, with no horizon and no visibility, so that Lyon had been unable to take a sextant sight of any stars during a lengthy period when we had been circling, climbing, banking and turning.

The truth is that at this part of the flight we were not at all certain where we were; we did not know how much farther we had to go to reach Suva, and I began to worry about our petrol supply again. We had now been 12 hours in the air; it was 10 am, and we had petrol for seven hours left.

I had had a long and tiring night, and handed over the controls to Ulm while I fell into an unsatisfying doze. I felt I could sleep for hours, but I was soon jolted awake again by a sudden change of course. It brought me to my feet.

I began to swear at Ulm for falling asleep while at the controls, but he was grinning and pointing with his hand.

My gaze followed the direction in which he was pointing. No wonder Ulm had a happy grin on his face.

I saw a smudge low down on the horizon. It was land – one of the Fiji islands.

But which?

There is a whole bunch of the Fiji's, and it was quite impossible for Lyon to determine which one this was until he had been able to check our latitude and longitude by means of a sight.

We therefore brought the plane down lower and lower, until at length we were flying only 20 feet above the water. At this height we gave Lyon a visible horizon only a few miles away, so he was able to bring the reflected sun in the mirror of his sextant down to this line, and thus obtain a good altitude.

But while he was taking his sight we looked around for the island again.

It had disappeared!

I looked at Ulm, and Ulm looked at me.

This was really uncanny, for we had no doubt in our minds whatever that we had seen land. I had seen it, Ulm had seen it, and so had Warner and Lyon. We could not all have been mistaken, and yet now the island had disappeared completely.

The explanation was, of course, very simple, although it did not immediately occur to us. At the height at which we had first sighted the land, we had a range of vision of 70 or 80 miles. We could see far out over the curve of the globe, but as soon as we began to drop, our range of visibility began to be restricted, owing to the curvature of the earth.

Lyon managed to get a very good sight, and was able to fix our position with some degree of certitude. We found that the island in sight was Exploring Island, which is in longitude 179 west.

Soon after we crossed the international date line and dropped a day out of our reckoning, and passed from Sunday to Tuesday.

We were now at a good altitude again, and looking out for Suva. We were all in good spirits. Our goal was in sight. We knew where we were. The three engines were roaring away, as usual, and we still had ample petrol remaining.

But these long distance flights are not accomplished without a succession of trials and anxieties, and I now began to think about our landing ground.

We had previously telegraphed to Suva, prior to leaving Oakland, for details of the Albert Park Sports Oval, which was the only suitable spot where we could land. The maximum runway, however, was barely 1200 feet, in addition to which there were some awkward telegraph poles, and three trees at the north-west corner which we had asked to be removed.

We were now in fairly light condition, but as we circled round Suva I anxiously looked out for the landing ground.

After over 30 hours in the air, I knew that I was not altogether as bright and sharpwitted as when we took off. The strain of the blind flying and the bombardment of the rainstorms had added to my fatigue, and, furthermore, I had never seen the Albert Park Ground.

As I came down, I suddenly caught sight of a steep drop of about 12 feet from the roadway to the field, and we were coming along at 65 miles an hour. We touched the ground halfway up the field. In front of me was a sharp rise, clothed in trees and thick undergrowth.

I had to ground loop the plane and swing away to the left as we came to a stop.

It was 3.50 pm. We had flown 3138 miles nonstop in 34½ hours.

As I stepped out to face the crowd, I had a feeling of exaltation, a sense of accomplishment.

The *Southern Cross* had made the longest non-stop ocean flight on record.

6 Lotus Land

Of course, we were stone deaf on arrival at Suva, and in no condition to answer the excited questions of the crowds of people who flocked round us. We were dazed and bewildered as we watched the frantic efforts of the Indian and Fijian police to drive the crowd back.

Through the lane formed by the united efforts of the police, a man approached me and held out his hand. 'I congratulate you,' he said. 'Will you all lunch with me tomorrow?'

'Yes. Isn't it?' I agreed.

He brought his face closer to mine, and said something. 'Excuse me,' I said. 'I didn't catch your name'.

There was some embarrassment and confusion. He laughed. I laughed.

We all laughed – but I did not know why I was laughing, unless, perhaps, it was the reaction from the strain.

Later, I found out the cause of the little contretemps. The man who had addressed me was His Excellency Sir Eyre Hutson, High Commissioner of the Western Pacific and Governor of Fiji, and he had been asking us all to lunch with him at Government House.

At last, secure in the knowledge that the police and defence forces were guarding our machine, we allowed ourselves to be dragged away to the hotel where a hot bath and food awaited us. Then sleep – glorious sleep. But at midnight I awoke, wondering about our takeoff wondering about the *Southern Cross*. Was she all right?

Ulm and I went out in borrowed kimonos to see. We reached the plane and stooped under the ropes, which surrounded the plane. As we did so, Fijian policemen appeared with rifles at the ready.

They could not speak English. They had orders that no one was to approach the plane; and our appearance at that hour, roaming round, was an added incentive to them to carry out their orders to the letter.

There was no doubt of the *Southern Cross* being safe. We returned to bed content.

There were four possible taking-off sites recommended by flying men at Suva. One was at Naselai Beach, some twenty miles away, and others a few miles from the town of Suva. We agreed that I should go in the Governor's launch *Andi Beti* (*Princess Elizabeth*) to inspect Naselai Beach, whilst Ulm inspected the other sites nearer Suva, and he, with Warner and Lyon, attended to numerous business and social details.

It is fitting here that I should acknowledge how much of the success of the flight was due to the ability and untiring efforts of my friend, Charles Ulm. From the time that he wrote the first letter to a Sydney newspaper setting out our plans, his organising ability was mainly responsible for our eventually commencing the flight.

He was co-commander, organiser and relief pilot of the whole of the expedition. Of a total of just over eighty flying hours on the trans-Pacific flight Ulm flew over 30 hours and I over 50 hours.

On arrival at the beach I was delighted to find that it formed an ideal takeoff – the best runway I had seen. The sand was firm and hard, and there was ample space, but it was 20 miles from Suva, and all our petrol would have to be transported there by launch.

We were in a hurry to get on. We had pledged ourselves to dine in Sydney on Saturday night, and this was Wednesday. Our many kind friends in Suva hastened the preparations on our behalf. The petrol supply was loaded up in the launch *Pioneer*, which set off for the beach.

The following morning (Thursday, 7 June) we said goodbye to Suva, prior to flying the *Southern Cross* to Naselai.

Thousands had come in from the outlying villages. They had never seen a plane before. The *Southern Cross* impressed and overawed them. They composed ballads lauding the 'bird ship', and gathered round her in thousands as Ulm and I stepped in to take off for Naselai.

It was only a short trip, and as we only had 85 gallons on board, and had left Warner and Lyon to come over by launch, we had no difficulty in taking off from the Albert Park ground after a short run of 400 yards.

Naselai is the home of a tribe whose small domain had never before been invaded by an aeroplane. We wanted their services for the loading of the plane at Naselai was no easy task.

Great rollers burst into foam as they crashed on the beach. The tide had been driven back by a strong south-east breeze, and the surf was roaring on the beach in a cauldron of foam almost up to the line of palm trees which fringed the coast.

The *Pioneer* was unable to come in close, but was obliged to stand off nearly a mile from the shore while the petrol, in 40-gallon drums, was discharged into surf boats, whose crews cleverly made their way in to the beach and rolled the drums into the surf, whence they were dragged ashore.

Until the tide ebbed and left the beach clear for us, we could not land, and consequently we were obliged to remain in the air. We flew back to Suva, where our appearance caused some consternation, and then we aimlessly flew around, killing time until the tide had ebbed sufficiently to allow me to make the landing on the beach, after which the drums of petrol were brought ashore through the surf, and our tanks slowly filled.

The delay was irritating in the extreme. I realised that we should not get away that day. Yesterday we had no doubts that we should be able to 'fly away' on the morrow. Now the morrow had come – and gone.

We decided to spend the night in the *Pioneer*, and reached it through the surf, wet through. Lyon had joined us, but Warner stayed on the beach for the night and what a night he had!

Next morning we discovered that he had slept in a Naselai village; he had drunk of the sacred Yangonga ceremonial drink and he had been initiated into the tribe.

We spent the morning hours of Friday, June 8, lolling on the deck of the *Pioneer* watching the palms, the sand, the blue water, and the Fijians. We could not take off till the afternoon when the tide ebbed. It was a forced leisure and we thoroughly enjoyed our brief spell in this Lotus Land, 'where it was always afternoon . . . where the very air did swoon'.

Lyon, being a seaman, and therefore superstitious, pointed out that Friday was an unlucky day to start. We pooh-poohed his fears away. In any case, did we not carry a whale's tooth – the symbol of the Fijians' best wishes, which has been presented to me by the oldest Fijian, Rata Joni Mataitini, MLC?

We wheeled the plane down on to the smooth, hard sand and swung her in the right direction for the takeoff. The time had come to leave, when we were deeply touched by one of the most charming little ceremonies I have ever witnessed.

A party of Fijian maidens shyly approached us, each carrying a bowl of Yangonga, of which we partook. The chief of the tribe at their head explained that this was the ancient ceremony to speed the parting guest. We thanked them with a few words through an interpreter, and wished them farewell.

Then we said goodbye to half a dozen friends who had accompanied us to Naselai, climbed into the cockpit, warmed up the engines, and we were off.

With 900 gallons on board we lifted after a run of 1000 yards, and in another minute we were looking down on the little knot of people below us on the beach.

It was 3 pm.

7 HOME

And now we were off on the third, last and shortest lap of the three.

We were all in splendid spirits.

The rest at Naselai had done us good, our plane was in fine fettle, and within a few minutes of leaving the beach we were swooping once more over the white roofs of Suva that gleamed and flashed in the afternoon sun.

We were heading out to sea at 85 knots, bowling along at an altitude of 1500 feet, while the green island, with its white roofs, its palms, it surf haze and unbounded hospitality, soon faded on the horizon astern.

The weather outlook could not have been more favourable; the engines roared with the same flawless rhythm, and Brisbane was only 1700 miles away – a distance which seemed quite short to us now hardened veterans.

But on these long distance flights – as I have previously remarked – one can never assume that 'All is well' for more than ten minutes at a time.

Our happy smiles soon faded when Lyon passed through a note to us. It read: 'EIC out of action'. This was the earth inductor compass, the most valuable steering instrument we carried, and with which we were steering our courses.

It was our own fault – as such mishaps usually are. The Pacific Scientific Company had taken the trouble to cable us at Honolulu and Suva giving full instructions for the care of the instrument, but in the battle of getting the fuel on board through the surf at Naselai, we quite forgot to oil the instrument.

It was a blunder on our part, the only one we made during the whole flight.

Lyon spent a long time trying to get it right, but all to no purpose, and for the rest of the flight we were obliged to rely on the magnetic steering compasses.

Our navigator feared these were inaccurate since they were subject to the magnetic influence of small metal objects in the cabin, but fortunately the steering and aperiodic compasses agreed, and we had no cause for disquiet.

I climbed to 4000 feet for the night, and about 6.30 pm we settled down for the nocturnal watch, never imagining that we would have other than a fine night followed by a glorious dawn, from which we should emerge flying triumphantly over Brisbane.

We never made a bigger mistake in our lives. Old Ocean had not done with us yet.

It was soon after seven o'clock that I began to realize that the conditions were changing. It grew colder and colder. The moon disappeared and the darkness closed down on us.

The visibility, which a short time before had enabled us to see the distant horizon, dwindled to a mile, then a few yards, then to nothing. Strong gusts rocked the plane about, giving us no peace; the torrential rain began to drum and rattle on the windshield.

We were peering out at a rushing cascade of water; we were enfolded in blackness. Our wet propellers glistened in the lash of the storm, reflecting the indirect light from the little bulb on the instrument board.

I began to climb to try and get above it.

We bumped and dropped and bucked; and raking gusts jolted the plane so that we had to hang on to our seats; but always the engines drove the *Southern Cross* steadily upward as we tried to escape from this blinding chaos of wind and water.

We had risen over 7000 feet, and still there was no relief. This was blind flying with a vengeance, and to add to my mental discomfort, the glass windshields began to succumb at their frames to the terrific pressure of the driving rain.

First came a steady drip on our knees, then a shower, and often a cascade, so that our overalls were soon sodden. As we climbed, it became colder until the blasts of wind became positively icy.

It was far worse than flying through the ordinary darkness of the night. We were tearing through a black chaos of rain and cloud at 85 knots, and our very speed increased the latent fury of the storm until it became an active and violent enemy which seemed to rush on us in an endeavour utterly to devour us.

This was a tropical deluge such as we had never experienced in our lives.

Lightning added fresh terrors to the night. It ripped a hole in the clouds, revealed great masses of black nimbus cloud and shot across the sky in awe inspiring jags.

It was an electrical storm and soon a crackle of blue flame played a little eerily round the plug leads on all three motors. The constant flooding of the spark-plug wires and the heavy electrical charge in the atmosphere caused these spurts of flame, and we began to reflect on the condition of our magnetos. If they were thoroughly wet, too, they might give out at any moment. It was a disturbing thought.

Meantime, we plunged on with no idea whatever of where we were. Any attempt at navigation was useless in these circumstances. We were circling, plunging, climbing, dodging the squalls and hanging on to our seat as the poor old *Southern Cross* pitched and tossed wildly about.

This was more than blind flying – it was 'stone blind'. All I could do was to try and keep the ship on an even keel, ease the strain as much as possible and remain in the air.

For four solid hours, from eight until midnight, we endured these terrible conditions, but soon after midnight I began to hope that we were beginning to run out of the worst of the storm.

I descended to 4000 feet.

The electrical charging seemed to have passed, and though we dodged and twisted in efforts to keep clear of the rain it was much lighter, though the bumps were if anything worse than ever.

Rain, rain, rain! How sick we were of rain that night.

Time after time we thought we saw it clearing ahead. Sometimes we could catch a glimpse of a star but inevitably those heavy black curtains would be drawn again and we would plunge blindly into more rain.

About 4 am we came down to 1400 feet to try and economise fuel. Our limbs were stiff, our hands so numb that the fingers couldn't hold a pencil. The log which Ulm was keeping shows no entries from 6.15 pm to 3.20 am. except for a brief description of the storm about eleven o'clock that night.

But, as is usually the case, the dawn brought an improvement. We seemed to be leaving the storm behind us; the rain eased off, but the sky had a heavy sodden appearance, and the sea was a sheet of lead, grey and forbidding.

By 7 am conditions had so much improved that Warner tried to pick up a radio bearing from Brisbane, while Lyon took a sight, and we altered our course to 270 degrees, which is due west. In other words, we considered we were on the parallel of Brisbane.

Our goal was surely in sight.

As the minutes passed we were all impatience to sight the coast of Australia. The sun warmed the air, our numbed hands came to life again, but our frozen feet remained frozen.

As we sped on, four pairs of eyes anxiously scanned the distant horizon.

The visibility was now very good. We could see the horizon like a clearcut line. A vague greyness seemed to merge with the cobalt-blue of the sea.

It was a shadow. It was a cloud.

It was not a cloud!

As we approached it at over 70 knots, it assumed more definite form.

Land!

It was the Australian coast!

But what part of that long coastline had we struck? As we drew nearer we saw no sign of Moreton Island, the airman's landmark for Brisbane.

We swept in over Ballina. We were, 110 miles south of our course.

There were two simple reasons for this great divergence.

First, the fact that the earth inductor compass had been out of action since we left Naselai, and secondly, the storm had blown us clean out of our course. Between 9 pm and 2 am we had been flying blind, with no hope of navigation, which was out of the question.

We sped up the coast towards Brisbane. The sun shone warmly as we approached Eagle Farm aerodrome, where a crowd of 15 000 had gathered.

As we glided down at 10.13 am a police inspector tried to restrain the crowd.

'Get back!' he shouted. 'Get back! This is no ordinary plane.'

That police inspector was right. The *Southern Cross* was no ordinary plane.

What a wonderful old ship she had been! She had borne us in safety over 7389 miles of ocean; her three engines had revolved without a fault over 24 000 000 times; she had lifted the heaviest burdens we could place on her; she had flown safely through the fiercest storms and blinding rain; she had answered every call; she had not failed us once and she had herself come through unscathed.

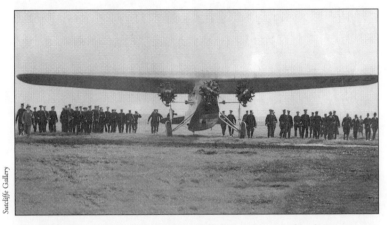

Sutcliffe Gallery

'Get back! This is no ordinary plane.' Southern Cross with police escort at Brisbane.

Photographer Unknown Southern Cross Trans Pacific Flight

'This was a feat which ... would bring fame to our country.' Smithy and Ulm in Sydney.

'... we looked down on an ocean of heads ...'

'... what shall I say of the amazing spectacle that greeted our eyes?'

If our reception in the capital city of Queensland on Saturday was almost overwhelming, what shall I say of the amazing spectacle that greeted our eyes as we flew over the harbour and city of Sydney?

It seemed as if the entire population of Sydney had either assembled at the Mascot aerodrome, or was on its way there.

It was a Sunday afternoon, and we had expected a quiet little crowd of 10 000. Instead, we looked down on an ocean of heads, which I am told numbered 300 000.

The *Southern Cross* had indeed come home!

Kingsford Smith
WINIFRED TENNANT

Ask the sun; it has watched him pass –
A shadow mirrored on seas of glass;
Ask the stars that he knew so well
If they beheld where a bird-man fell.
Ask the wind that has blown with him
Over the edge of the ocean's rim,
Far from the charted haunts of men,
To the utmost limits and back again.
Ask the clouds on the mountain height,
The echoes that followed him in his flight,
The thunder that prowls the midnight sky,
If a silvered 'plane went riding by.

If the birds could talk, would they tell of the fall
Of a god who winged above them all?
Of an eagle-man, by the world's decrees,
King of the blue immensities?

EDITORS' NOTE: Charles Kingsford Smith and Tom Pethybridge left England on 6 November 1935 attempting to break the record to Australia in the *Lady Southern Cross*, a Lockheed Altair single-engined aircraft. Smithy had not been well for some time and suffered severe headaches during the two-day flight to Allahabad. The next day Jim Melrose, who was engaged in an attempt to break the solo Britain to Australia record, sighted the *Lady Southern Cross* over the Bay of Bengal.

'I could see jets of flame spurting from Smithy's plane's exhaust pipe,' Melrose said, 'and I was overcome by an eerie sensation as I watched.'

Despite a huge search no trace was ever found of *Lady Southern Cross*.

'King of the blue immensities ...' Smithy.

Hinkler, Hinkler, Little Star

Jim Haynes

Hinkler, Hinkler, Little Star
16 days and Here You Are

As a boy in his home town of Bundaberg in Queensland, Bert Hinkler spent hours watching ibises fly. From early childhood Hinkler had just one ambition: to spend his life flying. As a teenager he built gliders, modelled on the ibis. When he was twenty he left home and headed to Richmond, near Sydney, where he washed down the plane making joyride flights over Sydney every night in return for just one flight. Unfortunately his mother followed him from Bundaberg and prevented him from having his first flight.

But nothing could stop Hinkler. There were no flying schools in Australia so he worked his passage on a freighter to Germany, when still only twenty, and made his way to London, where he eventually landed a job as a mechanic with the Sopwith aircraft company. When war came, he joined the Royal Naval Air Service as an observer, won the Distinguished Service Medal, gained a commission, and joined the Royal Flying Corps.

Bert Hinkler flew into history in February 1928, when he piloted an Avro Avian from London to Darwin in fifteen and a half days, smashing the record of twenty-eight days for the journey. It was the longest solo flight ever made.

Hinkler flew the 1100 miles non-stop from London to Rome, a first leg which demonstrated his determination. He continued flying long stages every day, with a regularity that made it seem inevitable that he would achieve his goal.

Hinkler's rapid progress and endurance seemed incredible at the time. He was small of stature and quiet and modest by nature, but he was physically strong and was a gifted and expert pilot with thousands of hours experience testing aircraft.

From Rome he flew to Malta direct, then crossed the sea to Benghazi the next day and followed the North African coast to Tobruk that afternoon. Three days from England to the continent of Africa was a record at that time.

On 11 February, Hinkler flew from Tobruk to Palestine. The next day he set off for Baghdad, but made such good time that he kept on to Basra, covering 950 miles in a non-stop flight of nine and half hours.

On 14 February, after a flight in beautiful weather down the Persian Gulf, the Avro Avian landed in Karachi, seven days after leaving England. This established a new record. Five thousand miles had been flown in seven days at an average of over 650 miles per day.

The fastest normal travel time from London to the edge of the Empire at Karachi was then about three weeks, by train and ocean liner. The idea that this could be reduced to less than a week was a source of wonderment to the expatriates, colonial officers and civil servants who suddenly began to think of the possibility of being able to read English newspapers only a week old.

The only problem experienced up to this time was a slight leak in an oil tank, which Hinkler discovered as he flew down the

Persian Gulf. This was was quickly repaired by RAF mechanics and caused no real delay to the flight schedule.

As Hinkler crossed India in two stages, from Karachi to Cawnpore and from Cawnpore to Calcutta, he passed the halfway point of his journey. It took him just two days to cross the subcontinent.

On the next stage to Rangoon, Hinkler encountered the first really bad flying conditions of the trip when he was forced to fly through two tropical storms and heavy rain. Rangoon to Burma was a relatively uneventful stage but, on the next day, on the stretch to Singapore, he again struck several heavy rainstorms and, just before reaching Singapore, he found it necessary to make a wide detour to miss a thick storm belt.

From Singapore, Hinkler flew on to Bandung, in Java, on 20 February, and the following day he brought the Avian to Bima, his last stop before facing the final stage, across the Timor Sea to Darwin.

That night Hinkler tried to get as much sleep as he could in a native hut, but mosquitoes kept him awake and tropical rain pelted down.

At dawn he took off, with just a drink of water for breakfast and no food or water on board. Darwin was still 1000 miles away as he climbed with great difficulty through the turbulent tropical air and over the mountains to the south of the landing place at Bima.

For most of the stage across the open seas, clouds gave him some anxiety, but he maintained an altitude of 2000 feet, and a speed of 92 mph. Despite no visibility for most of the flight, Hinkler's compass reckoning proved very accurate, and he sighted the coast of Australia at 4 pm on 22 February.

He then followed the coast to Darwin.

The pioneer airman came in over the jungle to Darwin and circled the Ross Smith Memorial twice. He landed at Fanny Bay, 3 miles from the town, just after 6 pm local time.

A rather sunburnt, and very tired, Bert Hinkler gave a speech that evening at a civic dinner in his honour. In the speech a

Photographer Unknown Flight Magazine

'... he piloted an Avro Avian from London to Darwin.' Bert Hinkler and his Avian.

typically modest and unpretentious Hinkler said that the most critical day of the whole trip was the first, when he flew for three hours in darkness before reaching Rome, and his only real moment of anxiety was when fading daylight caused a forced landing in the North African desert and some rather menacing 'natives' approached him, but a gift of cigarettes solved the problem.

The King sent the following message:

> 'Please inform Mr. Hinkler that I have received the news of his safe arrival in Australia with great pleasure. I have personally watched the progress of the great flight with great interest and am delighted that it has been successful.'

Australia went Hinkler crazy. The government sent a cruiser to stand by as Hinkler flew his final leg, across the Timor Sea. Composers wrote songs about him, the nation's hit tune was briefly 'Hustling Hinkler'. People wore Hinkler buttons, girls wore Hinkler flying helmet type hats, Federal Parliament stopped to welcome him, the Queensland government gave him £500 and the Australian government £2000, plus the Air Force Cross and the honorary rank of squadron leader in the Royal Australian Air Force.

Bert Hinkler never used the rank or wore the uniform.

Hinkler later returned to England and invested his money in a company making aircraft named after the bird he used to study, the ibis. He flew the Atlantic from east to west, which was considered to be the greatest piece of solo navigation in aviation history.

On 7 January 1933, Bert Hinkler took off from London in an attempt to break his own record to Australia. It was the last flight of his career. Hinkler's body and plane were finally found in a remote part of the Italian Apennines in Tuscany at the end of April.

The Aero Club of Florence and the Italian government gave Hinkler a hero's funeral. He is buried in the English Cemetery in Florence.

The Singing Ace

C. J. Dennis

Utterly fearless, small, active, and with a schoolboy
grin, Hinkler (now crossing the Timor Sea on his final
hop) is an ideal long-distance flier. He has unique
endurance, enabling him to make a solitary flight for
hours, singing as the mood moves him. – The London
Daily Mail

There's an Aussie in an Avian high o'er the Timor Sea,
Flying on and singing as he flies
For the honor of his country, for the sake of you and me,
And the spirit, true and bold, that never dies.
He is speeding, he is singing, as the boys in old days sang
When the High Adventure beckoned them along,
Where the frowning cliffs of Anzac to their lilting voices rang,
And the crags of Sari Bair gave back their song.

There's an Aussie in the zenith where the Timor spills its flood.
Alone with sea and sky, he rides the air.
He is homing to his own land with her spirit in his blood,
And only sea-birds mark his passing there.
But he's singing, gaily singing with a heart aflame with hope,
And his eyes fixed on the far horizon's rim
Where tropic skies to tropic seas in azure glory slope
And the nearing shores of Homeland beckon him.

Where the Timor basks in sunlight there's an Aussie all alone –
Alone with sea and sky – a speeding mite,
Who flies o'er Asian seaways as no other man has flown
And finds but true adventure in the flight.
And he's singing – still he's singing, while the nations
breathless wait

And count the hours of waiting all too long,
Till he ends his long adventuring beside his mother's gate
And his kinsmen catch the burden of his song.

There's an Aussie in an Avian – a speck within the blue –
Who puts to shame old tales of fabled ships.
For honor of his land he sails, for proof for me and you
Who wait with greeting trembling on the lips.
And he's singing – ever singing as he drops the leagues behind –
The man who ventured half a world to roam,
And thankfulness shall mingle with the welcome he will find
When at last the Singing Ace comes winging home.

EDITORS' NOTE: Published in the *Melbourne Herald* Wednesday 22 February 1928. Hinkler arrived in Darwin at 6pm that day.

Out of the Blue

C. J. DENNIS

Speaking in welcome of the famous airman, Bert
Hinkler, yesterday, the Premier, Mr Hogan, said 'Today
Mr Hinkler has come to us out of the blue'.

Out of the blue. A glimmering speck
Draws on while the thousands cheer,
With straining vision, with craning neck,
Each one fearing he yet may wreck,
They gaze as his ship looms near,
Bringing, from half a world away,
Something to each man here today.

More than honor and more than fame,
More than a triumphing song
More than the tale of a well-won name.
More than the title of high acclaim,
Brings he to the clustering throng.
'Tis Vision, and Pride, and a Hope that's new
He brings with him shimmering out of the blue.

Strange, vague promptings of waxing Pride,
Vison for me and you.
Men who yet never may learn to ride
Into the void o'er a whole world wide,
Venturing into the blue –
Yet in the bosom of every one
Comes hope, because of a deed well done.

Is it that we of the age and race
Into which he was born
Seers for the moment, only trace
Something there of a hidden grace
Salve for a world forlorn?
As a sign and a portent of places new
Comes he thus winging it out of the blue?

Doubly an 'Ace' in that he, alone,
Played for the stake and won.
By such high deeds have the seeds been sown
Out of which Empire and glory have grown:
Thus are new worlds begun.
Was it something of this that we sensed today
When out of the blue he came winging his way?

Comes a new era for men of the earth
That the 'Lone Ace' flies this way?
Cook, Columbus were men of worth,
Drake knew much of the wide world's girth –
But night has followed their day:
A night of blackness that gave men fear,
When the gods of war strode all too near.

'Tis but the Dawn. Yet skies grow clear,
And the new Day breaks full fair.
But, as year follows on glorious year,
And the 'Tale of the Air' is an old tale here,
The name of Hinkler, Pioneer,
Shall shine while the skies are there –
Writ indelibly into the Blue –
'This Boy who had made his dreams come true'.

EDITORS' NOTE: Published in the *Melbourne Herald* 19 March 1928.

'This Boy who had made his dreams come true.' Bert Hinkler.

Melbourne Herald 19 March 1928

Pulling the Strings

'Thus are new worlds begun.' A cartoon of the time showing Hinkler
bringing the UK closer to Australia.

She's There

Jillian Dellit

She wasn't an Australian. The girl from Hull visited Australia only once and died a very English death, crashing into the Thames Estuary in 1941 while ferrying planes from the factory to RAF bases to support the British war effort.

Yet there is an enduring Australian connection. Every year in her home town, the Mayor of Hull presents a gold trophy to recognise the bravery of a local child. The gold cup was purchased by Amy Johnson with funds raised by the children of Sydney in honour of Amy's arrival 'down under' in 1930.

As a young woman, Amy Johnson spread out a map of the world, pointed to the uncharted spaces of the large open country in the Southern Ocean that was Australia and said, 'I'm going there!'

No doubt others of her generation had done the same. The difference was, Amy Johnson fixed her mind on this goal and worked until she reached it. In the process she altered forever the way Australians viewed that map.

Amy left Hull's Boulevard Secondary School in 1922. With first class honours in Latin in the Oxford Senior Local Examination, she went to Sheffield University to become a teacher.

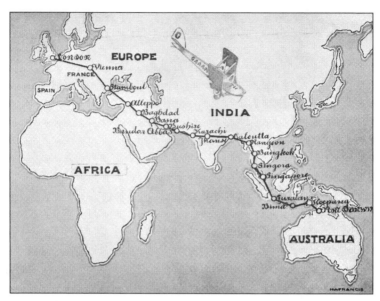

'*I'm going there.....*' Map of Amy's flight.

At Sheffield, Amy changed her mind, graduated as a Bachelor of Arts, went to London as a private secretary with a law practice and spent her spare time working in the field that had become her obsession, aviation. Each day, when her law firm job was finished, she did voluntary work at Astor House in Aldwych, the office of the Air League of the British Empire. In 1928 she joined the London Aeroplane Club and learned to fly.

She became seriously interested in aero-engines. Basic engine work was covered in the initial, Class A, pilot's licence. For most amateur pilots, like most car drivers, this elementary knowledge was all the formal mechanics they wanted.

Amy, however, was as smart with engines as she was with flying and cribbed time to strip, clean and mount engines with other members of the mechanics section of the Aero Club at their Stag Lane workshops.

To get the ground engineer's licence, she worked on planes after work for as long as the workshop would stay open, then was back again at six the next morning to put in another hour and a half before she had to get to the law office. She knew and understood every part of the plane and its engine, trusting her work with her life, test flying the planes she had worked on.

Here is Amy's own account of an average day in the workshops, written for the magazine *Air*:

Seven forty-five a.m.!

'Good morning' – me, brightly

'You're late,' – Boss boomingly: 'We start work at 7.30 sharp. You'll not put a foot inside this hangar to-day. You can go right home again.' (This is delivered in an 'engineer's choicest,' but I thought I'd better translate it.)

'Sorry, I'll never be late no more!'

I slip round the hangar door. Up comes a huge gum-boot and my leather coat behind takes on a slightly muddier look than usual. But I'm inside. On with the overalls – slightly soiled, I'm afraid – and up the steps I go, armed with grease gun, oil squirt, spanner, and the like, for an engine waits my personal attention. First I wash it down – with every minute the engine grows cleaner and I dirtier!

Tug-tug-tug – petrol filters do so object to being unscrewed! There! I've knocked flat the last of my once-pointed finger nails.

'Hoi, mate, Help,' shout I to my overall-covered neighbour up the steps at the next machine.

''Elp yerself to a bigger spanner!'

Most obliging and encouraging.

A large spanner somehow drops from my engine. I watch it get larger and heavier all the way down from the top of the engine, right down to the big toe of the Boss's foot! Wonderful rhetoric bursts from his lips! Suddenly he stops and turns to me as I listen in awe, wondering for the hundredth time when I shall be proficient enough to be awarded the engineer's licence!

'Did you catch any of that?'

'Oh no, I didn't hear a word! I must be more careful, you said?'

My, but I'm hungry. Landladies don't cater for breakfast at 7 am Hurrah, it's time for our cup of tea. In we all troop to the kitchen and take up our stand round the table. A huge cup of tea and thick cheese roll refresh and strengthen us for the rest of the morning's work.

Back roll the hangar doors and a procession of six yellow machines, each tail hoisted high on the shoulder of a mechanic, marches out on the tarmac. 'Props' are swung, and engines are left to warm up. Meanwhile I don scarf and cap, ready for running up my engine, for it's some cold job. Then over to the petrol pump, the machine must be taxied, and back again to the sheds, where I line it up with the rest – all awaiting for the arrival of the two instructors for test at 10 am.

One part of the day's work over. A boy is detailed to stay out on the aerodrome to start machines, look after the members' comfort (i.e. supply them with cushions, etc.), and the rest of us, Engineer No. 1, Engineer No. 2, (a boy and I) return to the hangar for our instructions.

'Jim – get on with those pistons. We're overhauling an engine in the engine shop.'

' John,' (that's me), ' sweep out the hangar and tidy up the office.'

Ugh, I thought I'd fled from housework to learn engines. But Engineer No. 1's word is law; so, armed with a broom bigger than myself, I set to work. The hangar has never before seemed so immense. Howsoever, patience is at last rewarded, and I reach the far corner (not to leave the rubbish there – I tried that once . . !).

My next job is to scrape carbon off a cylinder head. (Two of these should be finished in an afternoon, I'm told.) Mine looks like taking a week. Anyhow, it is dinner time before I have made any noticeable impression on its blackness. (The blackness, incidentally, has made a most notable impression on me!)

We have an hour for lunch, and it flies all too quickly in eating, joking and talking shop. The afternoon passes uneventfully, except for a newspaper man who arrives and asks to see the 'lady engineer'!

Everyone looks blank. No lady here. I emerge, rubbing dirty hands on the seat of my overalls, and join in the search. But when I wash my face and hands for tea, my secret is discovered.

'You want to know what I have done? No . . . ? Oh . . . what I wear!? Oh, I see. Well, I wear overalls over my clothes, and over my overalls oil, grease, dirt.'

But he's gone! He didn't seem to like the things I tell him! So away he trots to make it all up for himself.

Now comes a photographer. Oh hurry, where's my heart-shaped helmet, my manicure set and my powder puff. Where can my powder puff be? There's a spanner in my stern pocket, a few loose nuts, screws and bolts in every other pocket, but where, oh where, is my powder puff pocket? You see, I must look nice for the photographer, for I've been told that every pilot has several proposals weekly. So I must spread abroad my beauty!

I've had no proposals yet, so I suppose I'm no pilot. But while there's life there's hope. Maybe the stronger sex don't like my brawny fist . . . or brawny arm, is it? I don my smart flying suit and appear for once as others would have me be, but the minute the camera has clicked, off it comes . . . for in roll the machines to be put to bed for the night.

Hangar doors are closed, 'Good Nights' are all said, and off we go to our various pursuits.

Do I go to the pictures with my sweetheart? Oh no, indeed.

At 6 pm I have a lecture, and after that I hope to do some reading for my next examination. A hard life, but, by Jove – it's a good one !

If I didn't do it all voluntarily and for nothing I should, of course, consider I was grossly overworked, ill-treated,

*underfed and underpaid . . . but don't let the Boss hear this,
or I'll have to change this story to a 'Day as a Sacked
Engineer'!*

Amy became the only woman to hold a British ground engineer's
licence.

When Amy persisted with her idea of flying alone to Australia,
most experts were sceptical. It was not unusual for amateurs to get
their first licence on only eight hours of flight and crash the first
time they tried to fly any distance.

And this amateur was a woman, attempting to fly to Australia.
She had only been flying for two years and had clocked up less
than one hundred hours as a pilot.

Her attempts to interest newspapers, experts and officials in
sponsorship were unsuccessful. Tom Clarke, managing editor of
the *Daily News* and *Westminster Gazette* later told it this way:

> *Her scheme of flying to Australia alone stirred nobody to
> enthusiasm. It was first heard of towards the end of last year
> [1929], but no one could be got to aid with the financing of
> the project. To fly to Australia was not exactly original. And
> who was this obscure girl anyhow? Quite an ordinary person
> by all accounts. She could not be serious.*
>
> *Lord Wakefield was approached early in January. He felt it
> was a hopeless job for the girl to tackle. Miss Johnson next saw
> Mr. Fenton, the Australian Minister for Trade and Customs,
> who was visiting London. He patted her on the back as a
> kindly uncle would, and said: 'Go to Australia by steamer,
> my girl. You would be foolish to try to fly there.'*
>
> *Then she got in touch with Fleet Street through my
> Australian journalist friend. He rang me up one day in March
> and asked if we were sufficiently interested to assist with the
> financing of a flight to Australia by a young woman.*
>
> *So I said, 'Who is she? Anyhow, flying to Australia is not
> very original, and the last woman who went took months.'*

'Her name is Johnson. She means to do it – and alone. She's her own mechanic. Will you see her?'

I was not impressed, but I wrote asking her to come to see me at any time to discuss the matter. I wanted to dissuade her. To have any responsibility for a young girl's going alone on such a perilous journey was not to my liking. She came one day when I was out. My secretary saw her, and has since given me the following note of their interview:

'The most noticeable thing about Miss Amy Johnson was her complete independence.' Ready to leave, May 5 1930.

'The most noticeable thing about Miss Amy Johnson was her complete independence. She said she did not want any newspaper publicity – she was making the trip for her own amusement, and if anyone cared to write about her in the papers – well, that was their affair. She had been told her venture was worth a lot of money to any paper who would buy it, but was not particularly interested; and she tossed her head with its long, swinging earrings.

'She is small and slight, blue eyed, fair haired, but with an air of strength and willpower – something almost masculine, given the lie by the earrings which continually thrust themselves on the notice. They seemed to be there for the purpose of accentuating each toss of the small, haughty head, and showing the determination of their owner. They said, in their nodding way, what Miss Johnson did not put in words:

'"You may not think much of me, but I'll show you I can do it."'

'... with an air of strength and willpower.' Amy works on her engine at Hendon.

We had one more letter from Miss Johnson, a rather delightfully petulant protest against the announcement of her project, in which she said:

'I am not 23, and my age is of no importance. The longest flight I have done is not 200 miles; anyhow London to Hull is only 147 miles by air. I am not making a high speed flight, and, although I have a large fuel capacity, I do not intend making 1000-mile non-stop hops. My ambition is not to surpass the record time set up by Mr. Hinkler – in fact, I am positively certain that his time cannot be surpassed in a light aeroplane. My route is not across France and Italy and I do not touch Egypt.'

I heard no more from her. We probably felt she would do a nice flight or two and then come down with some sort of trouble, and hurry back home.

Only one expert, Major Travers, the chief pilot of the London Aeroplane Club, watched her training and thought she'd do it, because, he said, 'She knows her job'.

As well as sponsorship, Amy looked for a better paying job in the aircraft industry. One she hoped to get was a demonstrator of a new aircraft designed by a young man, James Martin. He later went on to invent the ejector seat and set up his own aircraft company.

In 1929, however, his plane was still not ready for flight and Amy finally relied on savings from her £3 secretary's weekly wages for the flight. Lord Wakefield, head of the Wakefield-Castrol oil company and 'patron saint of civil aviation,' sponsored her by paying for petrol. Her father bought the plane and she paid for everything else.

At that time the most dangerous stage of flying from Britain to Australia was seen as the last stretch across the Timor Sea. Several aviators had died on the 900 lonely miles from Sumbawa to Darwin, out of sight of shipping and effective communications. Hinkler went missing there for several hours. Crossing the Timor Sea was the loneliest kind of flying.

As well as knowing her job, however, Amy Johnson had personal reserves of energy and spirit. In most respects she wasn't an average person. She was fit, a good swimmer, and able to box and wrestle. Few knew that she had followed her ground engineer's licence in 1929 with a full navigation licence in 1930. The slight girl with the earrings was a woman to be reckoned with.

She learned quickly and adapted to new ideas. Three days before she started from Croydon on 5 May, she reduced another risk by making use of a new technology.

Tropical storms might well be unavoidable once out of Europe. In a tropical storm, with her Gipsy Moth overloaded with fuel at every takeoff, she ran a high risk of an uncontrollable spin ending inevitably in death.

In the last few years, RAF pilots had saved their lives in similar conditions by the use of parachutes. Amy had never worn one, but she went to the manufacturer to ask for advice. They trained her in half an hour.

The seat-pack parachute she settled on was light – a mere 8 kg – specially fitted to her size. The harness fitted over her shoulders, round her waist and legs so it would brace her whole body against the opening shock. She wore it, using its body as a seat, all the time she flew.

Along with all the other things she was doing to prepare, she read books on navigation, building up a good knowledge and confidence enough to choose the most direct 11 500-mile route across Europe, via Vienna and Constantinople, over the Balkans.

This route was complicated by the need for visas and immigration clearances for landings in several European countries, which was why most pilots avoided it.

The only thing she failed to do in preparation was to make full load tests before her flight. This is probably the reason it took her two attempts to get off the ground when she left Croydon aerodrome on 5 May 1930.

Three people saw her off. James Martin was one of them. There were no speeches or publicity, just a farewell kiss for her father. The

Gipsy Moth started immediately, but she had not allowed herself enough distance for the weight of petrol she was carrying for the ten hours to Vienna. Cautiously, she slowed and turned round.

The second time she lifted off easily. Five machines from the London Aeroplane Club escorted her out over Surrey.

On that day few planes took off, due to reports of fog all the way to Cologne. Amy met rain at one stage but otherwise covered the 800 miles in fine weather, landing on Vienna's Aspern Aerodrome after just under ten hours' continuous flying.

The next day, Tuesday, 6 May, she left Vienna for Constantinople via Belgrade and Sofia, another 800 miles, with more good weather apart from some rainstorms over the Balkans. There was a crowd to welcome her, when, after another twelve hours of solo flying, she landed in what is now Istanbul.

Now the world was interested. Amy had never crossed the Channel before, or flown more than 200 miles in a straight line. When she repeated the performance the next day, people began to understand the extent of her determination and flying ability. Fleet Street had underestimated her.

Speed was her focus on the 550 miles to Aleppo, down the Bosphorus on the third day. When she arrived she had spent twenty-seven hours in the air and covered over 2000 miles in three days.

Then, in the 500-mile stretch across the desert to Baghdad, a sandstorm forced her down into the desert, where, for two hours she fought to hold the Gipsy Moth to the ground, piling her luggage against the machine's wheels to prevent the wind taking it. She did this with a revolver in her hand, in case of trouble. The revolver wasn't for show; Amy Johnson had learned to shoot and was an excellent shot.

Without having to use the gun she got underway when the storm subsided and made Baghdad by nightfall on her fourth day. Bert Hinkler's England to Australia light plane record that she had thought unbeatable looked like being smashed.

On the fifth day, in Basra and Bushire, the towns where most pilots put down as light failed, locals waited for Amy, but she passed them by, making it to Bandar Abbas, 830 miles along the Persian Gulf. On her sixth day, 10 May, she got to Karachi, breaking Hinkler's England to Karachi record of eight days.

To cut two days off his time for the 5000 miles between London and Karachi had been unthinkable and was not explained by her shorter route. She had beaten the record mile by mile.

In an age of records it was big news. Hull in particular recognised a home town hero.

Hull was an aviation town. With a flying club organised by the National Flying Services, it was one of the first English municipalities to have an aerodrome. The Royal Navy's torpedo planes and flying boats were built at an aircraft factory along the Humber and a few miles out of town – near Kingston-upon-Hull – the Airship Guarantee Company (with Vickers as its major shareholder) built the new R100 airship to the design and under the supervision of Barnes Wallis, later to find fame for his dam busting bouncing bomb in World War II. And in 1921, the airship R38 broke apart during a trial flight and fell in flames over Hull, killing forty-four of the forty-eight British and United States passengers on board – the first airship disaster after World War I.

So the people of Hull depended on aviation, understood its risks and recognised a pioneering achievement when they saw one.

Like it or not, Amy was now in a popular competition with Hinkler's record as she left Karachi for a 1000-mile leg to Allahabad, en route to Calcutta. Her personal, single minded focus on flying solo to the isolated country at the bottom of her atlas was now public property.

Then, after 700 miles as she neared Jhansi, she ran out of petrol, and had to put down there for the night. On the eighth day, 450 miles beyond Allahabad, she was in Calcutta, the halfway mark, 7000 miles from England and still two days ahead of Hinkler's time.

Beyond Calcutta, on the ninth day, in heavy rains and against strong headwinds, she faced the Arakan Yomas ranges, the lowest of Burma's western mountains. For a while she flew high – up to

12 000 feet – but as the day drew on and visibility deteriorated further she was flying at no more than 150 feet first above the coastline and then the railway line, in order to find Rangoon where the racecourse served as the flying field.

Anxious to find the racecourse, and unwittingly 12 mile short, she mistook the playing field of Insein for the racecourse, but as it appeared too small she continued south. Today Insein is a suburb of Rangoon, home to Myanmar's only railway workshop and notorious for its prison; but, in 1930, it was a country town. So when Amy was unable to sight Rangoon, and with no visible alternative, she turned back to the playing field.

Once back over the Insein field, she brought the plane down square between the goal posts, only to run into a ditch and damage the Gipsy's undercarriage in the unmarked field. Fortune, in the form of the Government Technical Institute workshop right next to the field, came to her aid.

The repair time, however, eroded her good lead over Hinkler, and the media interest became more intense. It was now 13 May, her ninth day.

All 14 May, the local technicians helped repair the damage to the undercarriage and wing. She tore up army surplus shirts and used pink sticking plaster from the local chemist to repair the wing.

To test the repairs in the air she organised for the plane to be moved by road to the racecourse at Rangoon where she had the space she needed for take-off. She was losing time in this middle section of the journey.

On the morning of 16 May, as the good weather suddenly changed to heavy rain, she set off for Bangkok, 356 miles away.

From the coast, her course to Bangkok took her over treacherous mountains of rainforest where there was little chance of survival if forced to land. There was a passage through the ranges but many aviators had failed to find it. In the heavy rain she climbed to 10 000 feet, trying to fly blind over the peaks, and seeking clear patches. When she did find a clear patch, she was still on the western side of the range.

Keith and Ross Smith got through these ranges by going beyond 13 000 feet. In a Gipsy Moth this was not an option.

It took her seven hours to cover the route from Rangoon to Bangkok – a long time on your own with basic instruments in the mist and rain over mountains – but on the twelfth day, exhausted by her long struggle, and approximately level with Hinkler's time, Amy reached the Don Muang air force base in Bangkok.

She prepared her machine immediately for an early morning continuation towards Singapore. The keen, highly skilled Thai airmen helped. Their respect for her was based on their local knowledge of the terrain that she had conquered.

Down the Malay Peninsula on her thirteenth day she held the plane on course against headwinds and tropical rainstorms. Local radio networks followed her ragged progress. After six hours of flying, Amy was finally forced to land at Singora, modern Sonkhla, in southern Thailand.

Only on the following day was she in Singapore, looking happy at her reception. Two of Singapore's Gipsy Moth seaplanes escorted her in. The Singapore Royal Air force squadron operated Gipsy Moths, so this stopover could provide experienced aero-mechanics and the comfort of an aviation community.

It was her fourteenth day and she had now lost the contest for Hinkler's record. On her own terms, however, she had already performed miracles and at her present rate of progress she knew she would still arrive at Darwin in excellent time.

By now she was famous. People around the world followed her with intense interest, waiting for news of her arrival at the end of each long day of flying, anticipating the dangers of the final stage across the Timor Sea.

When pilots planned flights to Darwin they knew that the last hop of 1500 miles was the most risky for land planes. Fitting seaplane floats to the Gipsy Moth would have added another third to the cost of the plane – making it more than Amy could afford.

Before Amy set off, the local Singapore aviation club fitted a new bottom wing on her plane. Then she took off for Surabaya, hugging the edge of the Java Sea. Bad weather and fuel shortage forced her, after nine hours' flying, to use an emergency landing place. She was holding out to reach Samarang but eventually made a forced landing at a sugar plantation 60 miles short.

Local factory workers were quickly recruited to help patch the holes made in the Gipsy's wings by the sugar cane. The next morning, she found a better place for take-off, and with everything possible removed from the plane she flew out of the sugar and on to her chosen spot where the plane was reloaded for take-off to Samarang.

It was now her sixteenth day and, in the company of the Dutch mail plane, she barely touched down before heading for Surabaya, another 200 miles, where crowds came to watch her land. They wanted to see and touch this woman who defied their weather and terrain as the monsoons turned to the east. She seemed relaxed, showing no signs of the fatigue expected of a woman who had been flying alone for fifteen days.

Still, her priority was preparing her plane for the final, most feared stage of the journey. Attuned to the sound of her engine, she picked up an irregularity that alerted her to Magneto trouble. After Surabaya, she could expect no help if her engine failed. She had two long, dangerous sea stretches to go.

Bert Hinkler had crossed the Timor Sea at its widest part – 1000 miles from Bima on the island of Sumbawa – and locals assumed Amy too would land at Bima. They watched for her, but they had to be satisfied with a glimpse of her plane in the middle of the day. She did not land.

It looked as if she had chosen Atamboea, on Timor, as her last stop with its promise of a shorter sea flight to Darwin.

Then nothing. The watchers on the tiny islands, some with landing strips built in 1919 to help aviators in the first England to Australia air race, caught no glimpse of her.

Night fell around 5.30.

The Dutch administrators kept their communication system open. No news.

Local authorities prepared for a sea and land search. The government steamer, *Gemma*, was instructed to search the Timor Sea. Two flying boats were ready to start out from Surabaya.

First thing in the morning a telegram arrived from Amy.

She had landed in the village of Haliloelik, in Timor, 12 miles from Atamboea and the nearest telephone. She finally got herself into Atamboea late at night and found accommodation. In the morning she had to return to the village to fly her machine over to Atamboea aerodrome.

The whole world was waiting for that telegram.

The 'lone girl flyer' had come to stand for independence, hope, defying the odds, and a quiet refusal to accept imposed limits of distance, engineering, navigation or gender. Plenty thought she had proved a point and should stop before the Timor Sea, but Amy Johnson was not flying for the approval of others. She had come 10 000 miles to fly this last 500 miles, and fly it she would.

Radio listeners stayed tuned.

She left at dawn. Her only contact was about halfway over, when she sighted the Shell oil tanker, *Phorus*, which radioed her progress to Darwin. Several aircraft then set out to meet her.

The biggest crowd Darwin had ever recorded was waiting to welcome her.

It was 3.00 pm on 24 May, the nineteenth day of her journey. She was behind Hinkler's 1928 record time, but a week ahead of Ross and Keith Smith's time of 1919.

Amy's navigation and persistence had defied her critics. They could dismiss her pilot's licence, even discount her ground engineer's licence, but none of them had even considered the possibility that she might navigate so effectively and overcome every daily setback to reach Darwin.

Amy carried no wireless. She navigated the Timor Sea unerringly to Darwin using a compass and ruler. She had tuned the engine, strapped on her parachute and flown.

Over nineteen days the Gipsy's four-cylinder, air-cooled engine had proven reliable in rapid changes of temperature and almost constant service.

Like her engine, Amy had operated for nineteen days with little rest. Newspapers fully expected she would want to rest in Darwin for several weeks but within a few days she headed across the Northern Territory for Brisbane. On her arrival there, on 29 May, in a misunderstanding with an escort, she overshot the runway and the Gipsy Moth turned over, sustaining considerable damage. Amy escaped without injury, but the Gipsy Moth's flight ended in Brisbane.

When she flew into Sydney's Mascot airport, piloted by Jim Mollison, another British pioneer aviator, a group of Australian women pilots flew to meet and accompany her. Undaunted by discovering that they had accompanied the wrong plane, they took off and repeated the gesture!

Jim Mollison and Amy later married and competed as a team in the great centenary air race of 1934 before their eventual divorce.

Australia has a warm heart for heroes. Bundaberg had declared a holiday for local boy, Bert Hinkler, when he passed through. Darwin adopted Amy and did the same. The whole town, multicultural even then, turned out for the parade and speeches in order to catch sight of the young woman most experts thought would never make it.

On 24 May 1930 the world had changed. To Australians in particular, the future looked different. On every atlas the distance between our country and England was shrinking because a lone woman had determined to make it so.

Amy also showed us clearly that one, young, independent woman could succeed by following her own course mile by dogged mile against the indifference and patronising assumptions of much of the British establishment. And for that Australians loved her.

In every walk of life, even remote from aviation, people gave spontaneous applause to the gutsy 'lone girl flyer'.

King George V sent the following telegram:

The Queen and I are thankful and delighted to know of Miss Johnson's safe arrival in Australia, and heartily congratulate her upon her wonderful and courageous achievement.

The Australian prime minister, James Scullin, said, 'Heartiest congratulations on your achievement which has won the admiration of the world'. He invited Amy to attend a session of Parliament.

Tom Clarke, the managing editor of the *Daily News* and *Westminster Gazette*, who had been so dismissive before her flight, had the grace to apologise, noting wryly: 'Mr. Fenton (the Australian Minister of Trade and Customs) ... will meet her in his own country, to which he has gone by the steamer he advised for her'.

Perhaps the most fitting tributes were the London newspaper placards announcing her arrival in Darwin to the British public. Reflecting how personal the flight had become, the placards simply stated: 'SHE'S THERE'.

National Library of Australia (nla.pic-an24664499): Escort for Amy Johnson's landing in Sydney, June 4 1930.

'*Amy also showed us clearly that one, young, independent woman could succeed ...*'

Sutcliffe Gallery

'SHE'S THERE!' *Amy Johnson over the uncompleted Sydney Harbour Bridge in Kingsford Smith's* Southern Sun, *piloted by Jim Mollison and escorted by Smithy's* Southern Cross Midget.

Bibliography

Bird-Walton, Nancy, *My God It's A Woman*, Collins/Angus and Robertson, Sydney, 1990

Briggs, F & Harris, S, *Joysticks and Fiddlesticks*, Hutchison, London, 1930

Hayes, Mike, *Angry Skies*, ABC Books, Sydney, 2000

Kingsford Smith, Charles, *My Flying Life*, William Brendon and Son, Ltd. 1937

Kingsford Smith, Charles, *The Old Bus*, Herald and Weekly Times, Melbourne, 1936

Kingsford Smith, Charles, *The Southern Cross Trans-Pacific Flight*, Penlington and Somerville, Sydney, 1928

McNally, Ward, *The Man On The Twenty Dollar Note*, Reed, Sydney, 1970

Odgers, George, *Pictorial History of the Royal Australian Air Force*, Ure Smith, Sydney, 1965

Smith, Ross, *14,000 Miles Through The Air*, McMillan, New York, 1922

Smith, Ross, *From London to Australia by Aeroplane*, National Geographic, Washington, 1921

Stackhouse, John, *From The Dawn of Aviation – The Qantas Story*, Focus, Sydney, 1995

Acknowledgments

We are especially indebted to Mike Nelmes for his generous assistance with the Narromine story and photographs, research on flyer photographs from both World Wars and proof reading.

Nancy Bird-Walton, for her time and good-humoured assistance in proofreading, and for the photograph.

Special thanks to Ken Wright for the Michael Dicken story and the Mildura OTU history. Thanks also to Jim Dellit and Robyn McMillan, and the following:

For help with research
Mike Nelmes, Executive Officer, Office of Air Force History
Ken Wright, Historian, No 2 Operational Training Unit (OTU) Museum, Mildura
Dan McFarlane, Secretary, No 2 OTU Museum, Mildura
Peter Kierath at Narromine Aviation Museum
Laura J. Kissel, Curator Byrd Polar Research Center Archive Ohio State University
Office of Air Force History
Narromine Aviation Museum
No 2 Operational Training Unit Museum, Mildura

For help with photographs
Mike Nelmes
Ken Wright
Nancy Bird-Walton
Dan McFarlane, Secretary No 2 OTU Museum, Mildura
Laura J. Kissel, Curator Byrd Polar Research Center
Colin Sheehan, Sutcliffe Gallery
Alleyne Johnson, Qantas Founders' Outback Museum
Norma Scott Molloy at Australian Picture Library
Neil Smith, 3 Squadron Association webmaster
Joanne Murray, National Library of Australia

For photographic permissions
Nancy Bird-Walton
Australian Picture Library
Sutcliffe Gallery
Australian National Archives
National Library of Australia
Narromine Aviation Museum
No 2 Operational Training Unit Museum, Mildura
Qantas Founders' Outback Museum, Longreach
Vic Hall Collection, Narromine Aviation Museum
Sir Hubert Wilkins Collection, Byrd Polar Research Center
Archive Ohio State University
3 Squadron Association
Office of Air Force History

At ABC Books
Special thanks to: Helen Littleton, Brigitta Doyle, Stuart Neal
and Lauren McCorquodale.